CLEVELAND CALAMITIES

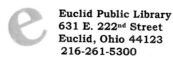

CLEVELAND CALAMITIES

A HISTORY OF STORM, FIRE AND PESTILENCE

ALAN DUTKA

Charleston   London

THE
History
PRESS

Published by The History Press
Charleston, SC 29403
www.historypress.net

Copyright © 2014 by Alan F. Dutka
All rights reserved

First published 2014

Manufactured in the United States

ISBN 978.1.62619.336.9

Library of Congress CIP data applied for.

CONTENTS

CONTENTS

PREFACE

One of my earliest memories of downtown Cleveland is the crunching sound created when I stepped on thousands of insects covering the city's sidewalks. On another childhood adventure, I accompanied my parents to the Yorktown Theater, where I experienced a large *pop* in my ears as the theater's doors blew open, heralding a storm described as the "devil wind." As an adult, after staging a Fourth of July cookout in 1969, an army of relatives returned to spend the night, unable to drive through a violent derecho.

On January 28, 1977, not listening to the morning news or weather forecasts, I drove to work accompanied by what I considered to be a fairly strong wind. Upon my arrival, a security guard informed me that the entire city had shut down and that I had just driven through the worst blizzard of the century. Nine years later, I thought I felt the earth move while driving through University Circle. Sure enough, Cleveland had experienced an earthquake centered in northeast Ohio.

The events helping to create these memories are described in this book, along with additional tales of floods, pseudo–tidal waves, a burning river, polio epidemics, environmental disasters, UFO sightings, a comet supposedly on target to poison the world, global cooling and a summer highlighted by a June blizzard. I hope that these stories, in addition to entertaining you, will enhance a few of your own memories.

ACKNOWLEDGEMENTS

The following individuals provided significant contributions to this book:

CLEVELAND PUBLIC LIBRARY
Beverly Austin (history)
Margaret Baughman (photographs)
Ronald Burdick (history)
Nicholas Durda (photographs)
Patrice Hamiter (photographs)
Sabrina Rosario (history)
Chris Wood (history)

CLEVELAND STATE UNIVERSITY
William C. Barrow (Special Collections)
William Becker (Archives)
Lynn M. Duchez Bycko (Special Collections)

GREAT LAKES BREWERY
Pat Conway
Marissa DeSantis

HEIDELBERG COLLEGE
Dr. Kenneth Krieger

Acknowledgements

The History Press
Greg Dumais
Ryan Finn
Savannah Brennan
Natasha Walsh
Katie Parry

Individuals
Alex Bevan
Diane Dutka
Priscilla Dutka
David Kubic
Ann Toth
Danielle Toth

Part I

WIND, RAIN, FUNNELS AND QUAKES

Extraordinary Blizzards

Clevelanders seem to be burdened with more than their fair share of heavy snow and strong winds, the two building blocks of blizzards. Nevertheless, prolonged wind exceeding thirty-five miles per hour combined with visibility of less than a quarter mile, an official definition of a blizzard, really isn't very common. And many of Cleveland's most notable blizzards have merely passed through the city on journeys engulfing significant portions of the United States. Yet blizzards have inspired tales of death, destruction, courage and valor that are entrenched in Cleveland's history.

On January 21, 1910, heavy snow and wind ignited a two-day blizzard that created havoc across the city. In the West Park neighborhood, freight train brakeman John W. Krantz fell from the ice-covered roof of a boxcar. Landing between two moving cars, the train's wheels crushed his body. In another incident, a set of freight cars jumped a snow-covered track, plunging down an embankment. The accident decapitated the conductor. At the intersection of East Fifty-fifth Street and Broadway Avenue, snow halted a Cleveland Railway funeral car destined for Calvary Cemetery. After crewmen worked unsuccessfully for an hour attempting to free the car, the funeral party completed its journey by transferring to several carriages supplied by a nearby funeral home.

The storm also provided a setting for quick thinking and consummate courage. Eleven-year-old Ben Eisenberg, selling newspapers on Public

Following a 1910 blizzard, Clevelanders helped shovel a sidewalk and road near East Ninth Street and Superior Avenue. *Courtesy of Cleveland Public Library, Photograph Collection.*

Square, spotted a runaway horse and carriage headed directly for a throng of terrified bystanders. As the horse passed, Ben leaped onto the wagon, bringing the carriage under control just before it reached the frightened crowd. Although the fourth grader worked four hours each evening selling newspapers, he had no intention of quitting school. Ben remarked, "A fellow can't do much unless he knows something."

Just a few weeks later, a remarkable blizzard started near the Pacific Coast. The storm moved relentlessly eastward for more than a week, passing through Cleveland on its way to Buffalo. Snow, beginning in Cleveland late on February 16, continued for two days. Forty-mile-per-hour winds formed ten-foot snowdrifts; dozens of barns, livery stables and other structures collapsed under the weight of the snow.

Snowdrifts in rural areas halted interurban traffic. Beached passengers received bread, butter and nuts but could not be quickly rescued because of the deep snow. A passing interurban killed a Lakewood woman on her way to church when she mistook the train's path for a sidewalk. On March 24, less than six weeks after the second Cleveland blizzard that season, straw hat and ice cream social weather returned as the temperature climbed to eighty-seven degrees.

Three weeks into 1913, Cleveland endured a snowstorm mixed with forty-eight-mile-per-hour winds. Two months later, blinding snow, a

Sandwiched between the blizzards of 1910 and 1913, two snowstorms battered Cleveland in 1911. Horses pulled snowplows to remove accumulated snow from Public Square. *Courtesy of Cleveland Public Library, Photograph Collection.*

piercing forty-mile-per-hour wind and ten-degree temperatures plunged the city into another blizzard. The storm hampered railroad employee Tony Corina from hearing or seeing an approaching slow-moving train. After hitting Corina, the conductor applied the train's brakes, pinning the workman under the wheels of the then-stopped train. These two furious storms later seemed almost inconsequential when compared with the great fall blizzard that year.

During the tempest of November 1913, the *Plain Dealer* portrayed the city as follows: "Cleveland lay in white and mighty solitude, mute and deaf to the outside world, a city of lonesome snowiness, storm-swept from end to end." Helen Keller, a guest at the Statler Hotel, described her experience in these words: "The rooms, the corridors, everywhere within this building, vibrates with the power of the storm outside." She further characterized the blizzard by saying, "I felt the wreckage of wires. I heard the city become still, like a crying baby suddenly hushed to sleep under the thick blanket of the crib. I heard traffic stop, the hum of businesses cease, men's shouts die away."

Two separate storms combined to create this gigantic three-day blizzard; the first arrived from the Canadian Northwest and the second from Georgia. Freezing rain in the morning hours of November 9 changed to sleet and snow. Cleveland registered a record 17.4-inch snowfall, easily

During the blizzard of November 1913, snow and heavy winds created an eerie scene on Public Square. *Courtesy of Special Collections, Michael Schwartz Library, Cleveland State University.*

In the 1913 blizzard, drivers traveling on East Eighty-seventh Street experienced difficulty manipulating through heavy snow. *Courtesy of Cleveland Public Library, Photograph Collection.*

Looking west on Superior Avenue from West Third Street, street cleaning crews removed snow generated by the 1913 blizzard. *Courtesy of Cleveland Public Library, Photograph Collection.*

smashing the old one-day mark of 13.0 inches set in 1896. For nine hours, winds remained in the fifty- to sixty-mile-per-hour range, gusting to seventy-nine miles per hour.

Several large buildings collapsed under the weight of the snow. More than three thousand utility poles fell from the fierce wind and heavy snow, ending electricity, telephone and telegraph service. The downed power lines electrocuted horses, stopped trolleys and prevented communication with the rest of the world. Downtown workers dodged falling power lines and shattered glass from broken windows. At the end of the workday, all available hotel rooms filled rapidly, forcing latecomers to sleep in lobbies or on hotel desks.

Streetcars lay trapped in mighty snowdrifts. One interurban, journeying between Cleveland and Chardon, stranded three hundred passengers for thirty hours. A stalled snowplow on Madison Avenue halted six automobiles behind it; the drivers remained in their cars from 9:00 p.m. until the next morning. Four hundred people spent the night in autos at Euclid Avenue and East Fifty-fifth Street. Horses, not the preferred means of transportation at the time, made a temporary but impressive comeback during the blizzard. In a triumph of animals over machinery, horses pulled numerous automobiles from snowdrifts. Fifty teams of horses, along with three hundred men, helped the city clear snow from streetcar intersections.

Criminals exploited the inability of police to respond to crimes. Robbers in Cleveland's downtown Lake View Park took watches and other belongings from disoriented people who had lost their way. But some would-be thieves demonstrated a severe lack of criminal fortitude. A grocer's wife foiled one attempted robbery at gunpoint by scaring the villain with loud screams. The unsuccessful thief fled in a waiting taxicab.

In an alley off downtown Cleveland's Eagle Street, a German Shepherd faithfully watched over his master, a sixty-eight-year-old Confederate soldier veteran, who lay frozen to death. After William Lambert collapsed in the storm, his eight-year companion dragged him to his front door and then stood guard for two days. The dog prevented police from examining the corpse, giving up his watch only when Lambert's son, whom the canine recognized, came to claim his father's body. The German Shepherd then followed an ambulance to a West Twenty-fifth Street morgue. Other deaths included a man blown from the roof of a Lake Shore Railroad boxcar and another electrocuted by a live wire while shoveling snow. An oncoming train killed a conductor checking the safety of the track.

Five years later, a 1918 blizzard traveled northward from Texas, colliding with an Arctic high-pressure front driving cold air southward from Canada. When the storm arrived in Cleveland, the temperature dropped in eight hours from a relatively normal thirty degrees to a bitter fifteen degrees below zero. Winds averaged thirty to fifty miles per hour the entire day. Ten to fifteen inches of snow accumulated, while fifteen-foot drifts covered houses and vehicles.

When snow halted trains and streetcars, sleds transported stranded passengers who may have otherwise froze to death. Low gas pressure, coupled with a lack of coal, made cooking and heating difficult if not impossible. People temporarily abandoned their cold homes to reside in heated movie theaters. The downtown Hippodrome Theater remained open two entire nights to accommodate those wishing to sleep in the heated building. Churches also housed citizens who could not obtain coal for home heat. In an era before plastic, milk could not be distributed because the necessary empty milk cans accumulated in homes unreachable because of the storm. Remarkably, during the following winter season, a total of only nine inches of snow fell in Cleveland.

The National Weather Service called the 1950 Thanksgiving blizzard a "land hurricane." An Arctic air mass collided with a low-pressure system

Looking west from East Seventy-fifth Street, Lexington Avenue provided an example of the virtually impossible driving conditions occurring during the 1950 blizzard. *Courtesy of Special Collections, Michael Schwartz Library, Cleveland State University.*

from Virginia to create a six-day storm dropping 22.1 inches of snow on Cleveland. A thirty-ton Sherman tank, patrolling the Memorial Shoreway, rescued stranded motorists, while bulldozers cleared roads. The Ohio National Guard used jeeps to transport people to hospitals and deliver food to rural homes. Throughout Ohio, buildings collapsed under the weight of heavy snow, while twenty-three people died during the storm. Clevelanders demonstrated a hearty resolve not to be beaten down by the storm. Neighbors used a sled to transport an expectant mother across the city's streets to a doctor waiting to deliver her child. A soon-to-be bride walked ten miles to the church, where the groom nervously awaited her arrival.

Ohio State University and the University of Michigan geared up for a Columbus football game, with the Big Ten football championship, and a subsequent trip to the Rose Bowl, resting on the game's outcome. Game day conditions featured snow, temperatures in single-digits and forty-mile-per-hour winds. A cancellation would have sent Ohio State to the Rose Bowl, but the Buckeyes, not wanting to back into the honor, requested the game be played. A crowd of 50,503 braved the storm to watch a contest known as the "Blizzard Bowl." Although Michigan gained only twenty-seven total yards and never obtained a first down, the minimal offense resulted in a 9–3 victory. Ohio State's lone field goal occurred

As supplies entered the city following the 1950 blizzard, residents purchased food and milk at specially dispatched vehicles, such as this milk truck on Coventry Road. *Courtesy of Cleveland Public Library, Photograph Collection.*

after the Buckeyes blocked one of Michigan's twenty-four punts. Ohio State punted twenty-one times; one of the blocked punts rolled out of the end zone for a Wolverine safety. Michigan later fell on another blocked punt in the end zone for a touchdown but missed the extra point.

On January 28, 1977, an Arctic front swept southward through the northern Great Plains into the Midwest. Cleveland's temperature dropped from twenty-six degrees at 8:30 a.m. to one degree at 10:30 a.m. By evening, the temperature had fallen to ten degrees below zero. Sixty-mile-per-hour wind gusts created wind chills approaching fifty degrees below zero. Although five-foot snowdrifts accumulated on the Memorial Shoreway, Cleveland officially registered only two to four inches of snow. In Lake Country's snowbelt, legendary high-wire walker Karl Wallenda performed for a PTA circus at Mentor High School. Discussing his drive on Route 2, Wallenda said, "I have never been so nervous on the high wire in my life as I was driving in the blizzard."

One year later, on January 26, two colliding storms created the worst blizzard in Cleveland history. One storm arrived from the Northern Plains and the other from the Mississippi Valley. Temperatures dropped from forty-

Blizzard conditions on the downtown eastbound Shoreway, opposite Burke Airport, were a prelude to Cleveland's great blizzard of 1978, which occurred a few weeks later. *Courtesy of Special Collections, Michael Schwartz Library, Cleveland State University.*

During the 1978 blizzard, cars seen here on Brookpark Road, between Rocky River Drive and Grayton Road, serve as examples of the thousands of stranded automobiles throughout the city. *Courtesy of Cleveland Public Library, Photograph Collection.*

four degrees at 3:40 a.m. to five degrees at 10:20 a.m. Eight inches of snow and sustained winds of fifty miles per hour blasted the city. Gusts reached eighty-two miles per hour, generating wind chills exceeding one hundred degrees below zero. Cleveland recorded the second-lowest air pressure reading in the continental U.S history, outside of a hurricane, when the barometer fell to 28.28 inches.

The fierce wind hurled a woman on Public Square fifteen feet before she landed under a bus waiting to pick up passengers. The wind then propelled a man attempting to rescue her into the street. Both survived the ordeal. The Ohio Turnpike closed from end to end for the only time in its history, remaining completely shut down for two days. A salt truck flipped over, depositing six tons of salt on the intersection of Woodhill Road and Quincy Avenue. The Ohio National Guard rescued five people suffering from exposure on Brookpark Road, taking them to the NASA Research Center for assistance. Meanwhile, a Cleveland television news crew trapped itself in a whiteout while conducting live coverage of the storm. The most amazing story of survival involved a truck driver who pulled his rig to the side of the road near Mansfield to rest. The snow and high winds created a massive snowdrift while he slept. The driver spent five days buried in the truck before rescuers arrived.

FEROCIOUS FUNNELS

Late spring and early summer tornadoes are nature's most violent tempests, powerful enough to uproot trees, destroy buildings and homes, convert otherwise harmless objects into missiles and cause violent death. Although tornadoes pack the most concentrated form of atmospheric energy on the planet, three-quarters of Cleveland's tornadoes have lasted less than fifteen minutes. The earliest record of an Ohio tornado dates back to an 1804 storm in Geauga County. Accounts of an 1842 Cleveland twister describe the storm as demolishing homes and barns while hurling hogs, geese and hens through the air.

Larger and stronger tornadoes have struck northeast Ohio, but none has been deadlier than the twister of June 28, 1924. The storm killed eighty-five people, seventy-two of them perishing in Lorain. Smashing through downtown Sandusky and Lorain on a late Saturday afternoon, the tornado would have killed even more people had it struck on a weekday. The twister touched down near the northern edge of Sandusky. Eight people died, including a railroad employee sandwiched between two freight cars blown together by the wind. A collapsing building caused a bookkeeper's death. The storm destroyed one hundred homes and twenty-five businesses while tossing six automobiles into the Sandusky Bay.

The tornado entered Lorain near a municipal bathhouse, killing eight people seeking refuge from the tempest. Downtown Lorain, the next

A 1924 tornado killed seventy-two people in Lorain while demolishing large sections of the city's downtown. *Courtesy of Cleveland Public Library, Photograph Collection.*

target, suffered damages throughout a thirty-five-block area. Fifteen people perished when the storm blasted the Lorain State Theater. After heaving a truck against the fourth story of a building, the tornado propelled eight automobiles into Lake Erie. Citizens of Lorain later identified personal objects retrieved from places as far as the Pennsylvania border. The storm generated all of Lorain's death and destruction within a span of 104 seconds. The tornado then traveled through Sheffield and continued into Avon, where three deaths occurred. Another person died when the storm moved into West Dover.

Northeast Ohio experienced three other tornadoes that day. The first struck Sandusky County and traveled eastward toward Castalia. Another formed over Huron Township in Erie County. The third touched down near Geauga Lake and traveled twenty miles across northern Portage County. This tornado killed three farmers in milking barns north of Mantua.

A 1943 tornado completely blew away the second story of a Cullen Drive home on Cleveland's southeast side. Setting its sights on Broadway Avenue, the storm propelled a moving automobile against a building, ripped

A 1943 tornado nearly jammed these two houses together on Hague Avenue, a street south of Lorain Road between West Sixty-seventh and West Seventy-third Streets. *Courtesy of Cleveland Public Library, Photograph Collection.*

Opposite, top: The 1953 tornado caused this destruction near the intersection of West Twenty-eighth Street and Franklin Avenue. *Courtesy of Cleveland Public Library, Photograph Collection.*

Opposite, bottom: In the aftermath of the 1953 tornado, a Clinton Avenue homeowner relaxed in what remained of his house. *Courtesy of Cleveland Public Library, Photograph Collection.*

the roof off another structure, hurled a large billboard through the air and temporarily curtailed war production by damaging three defense plants. As the tornado destroyed about one hundred homes and injured scores of people, resourceful bar patrons used candles and a lantern to aid their drinking. Near Medina, another windstorm killed two orphans sleeping in a barn that collapsed. An executive of Cleveland's Dairyman's Milk Company died on his farm near Oberlin when a tree fell on him.

A deadly 1953 tornado began in Lorain County, killing nine people as it cut a 12.5-mile path through Cleveland's west side. Live wires electrocuted two residents. Although a West Twenty-eighth Street apartment owner and his wife survived being hurled though a glass window as the building collapsed, five of the residents died. Two married couples, one attempting to protect their six-

month-old daughter, all perished. Nearby, a three-month-old boy, swept from his crib, sailed past five homes before being smashed against a garage. A seventy-year-old woman died as her back porch collapsed.

A piece of lumber just missed hitting a woman before it crashed through two walls of her home. An airborne billboard landed on a moving automobile, but the driver incurred no injuries. A seventeen-year-old boy slept through the entire storm while the wind blew off the roof of his home and destroyed the garage. The power failed in the maternity ward of Lutheran Hospital; three new babies entered the world by candlelight. The tornado then moved directly into downtown Cleveland. A building housing a truck-servicing business collapsed at East Eighteenth Street and St. Clair Avenue, hurling bricks, debris and a ten-thousand-pound truck-trailer into the street. A falling pole smashed the front display window of a Superior Avenue company. Looters quickly arrived downtown, but city officials prevented widespread plundering by ordering police to shoot thieves on sight. After ruining a street party on Short Vincent Avenue, the tornado traveled into Lake Erie near East Fortieth Street.

In 1983, a tornado touched ground in the backyard of a Broadview Heights home. The winds killed the fifty-nine-year-old female head of the house, blew off the home's roof, collapsed the garage, tore bricks off the house and left only one wall standing. A portion of another Broadview Heights home traveled one-eighth of a mile, landing near Interstate 77. Next, the tornado journeyed twelve miles across Broadview Heights, Bedford Heights, Walton Hills and Solon, killing three more people and completely destroying twenty-five homes.

FOURTH OF JULY MISERIES

The Fourth of July holiday epitomizes outdoor fun and festivity. Americans by the millions partake in picnics, sailing, canoeing, sports and evening fireworks viewing. But in Cleveland, Independence Day can be a dangerous time for outdoor activity.

On the evening of July 4, 1969, a storm system beginning in Lower Michigan moved across Lake Erie. Accompanied by powerful rain, winds gusting to one hundred miles per hour and intense lightning, the storm navigated a right turn into hundreds of boaters waiting for Edgewater Park's annual holiday fireworks extravaganza. While most boaters reached the shore safely, a few smashed against a break wall, but none sustained serious injuries. Nevertheless, tragedy awaited as the storm moved inland. In Lakewood Park, falling trees killed teenagers Dagmar Dolejs and Gretta Schwartz. At Edgewater Park, Kenneth Rogers; his fiancée, Debbie Bianchi; and twenty-three-year-old Mrs. Joann Geneva died in a similar manner. Samuel Butler lost his life attempting to remove a wire lying on his automobile, while another fallen wire electrocuted Elmer Wachhaus when he picked it from the sidewalk. In total, forty-two people in northeast Ohio died during the storm.

The storm system creating the 1969 holiday miseries is a prime example of a derecho, a band of fast-moving and long-lasting thunderstorms accompanied by very strong winds. Surprisingly, the occurrence of an Independence Day derecho in Cleveland is not a rare event. Since the great storm of 1969, these severe storm systems have struck on the July holiday weekend in 1977, 1980, 1999 and 2003. The 1977 storm started in Minnesota and ended in northern Ohio after traveling 800 miles in fourteen hours. The 1980 squall, beginning near Omaha, journeyed through northern Ohio before dissipating over Delaware and Maryland. The 1999 storm began in North Dakota. Although the heart of this storm system did not directly hit Cleveland, 60-mile-per-hour wind gusts blasted Lorain and Vermilion. A boater, whose fifteen-foot sailboat capsized in Lake Erie, described the storm as a wall of white water with hail, rain, wind and lightning. Two to three inches of rain fell within a two-hour period in Cleveland. In total, the derecho traveled 1,300 miles in twenty-two hours.

On Sunday, July 6, 2003, picnickers enjoyed a final day outdoors before beginning a new workweek. The Chagrin River's depth measured only three inches as four adults rested in the calm water. Suddenly, a four-foot wave carried three in the group downstream as the river swelled in size and intensity. Firefighters eventually rescued the trio, far from their original resting place. A derecho starting in Iowa created the river's rapid transformation. Heavy rain, strong winds and dangerous lightning hammered much of northeast Ohio that afternoon. Meanwhile, communities in Lorain and Medina received no rain whatsoever.

The powerful 2003 rainstorm system remained past the Fourth of July weekend. Monday brought another day of severe wind, rain and hail. During a Tuesday storm, a Scoutmaster in Lorain County ventured outside his tent to check on his troops. Less than one minute after leaving the tent, a tree crashed down, landing directly on his cot. The storm system traveled south, reaching Columbus. A toppled tree crashed through the newly renovated home of "Dr. Mike" Thompson, a motivational speaker and writer who encourages people to cope with life's problems. Thompson told the Associated Press, "This will be great material, don't you think?"

In addition to the Fourth of July storms, a tardy 1995 derecho arrived one week late. Beginning in eastern Montana, the storm battered northern Ohio with winds peaking at one hundred miles per hour. A falling tree in a Medina County campground killed one man. A Lake Erie boater died when his boat overturned near Lorain. Early that evening, an engaged couple departed Kelleys Island in a fourteen-foot speedboat. Thirty minutes into their trip back to Cleveland, the calm Lake Erie quickly turned fierce as the powerful storm arrived. The boat crashed in a vertical position, with only the bow above water. Stranded for nearly eight hours in the cold water, Tom Fox and Char Tallman clutched the bow and a rope in their attempt to remain alive. Concerned relatives reported them missing. In the dark early morning hours, a rescue helicopter crew dramatically saved the couple.

SHAKES AND SWAYS

In 1870, Clevelanders possessed little experience dealing with earthquakes. When an October 20 quake shook the city, one man, in the process of shaving, concluded that he must have attempted suicide when his hand moved from his face to his throat. Attributing this behavior to temporary insanity, he consulted a physician. Several female workers in the Garment (Warehouse) District fainted when the quake struck. Pessimists foresaw the complete burial of the city if the earthquake interacted with quicksand buried under Cleveland's surface.

Buildings in downtown Cleveland swayed about one foot to the east and west. Upper floors absorbed almost all of the shock, while the street level experienced nothing unusual. Hotel employees, working in first-floor lobbies, watched in bewilderment as streams of guests rushed downstairs to evacuate the buildings. Centered in Quebec, the tremor caused anxiety throughout eastern Canada, as well as westward to Iowa and southward to Virginia in the United States. The total area encompassed more than 1 million square miles.

In 1886, Cleveland experienced four distinct shocks. Once again, exits became hotels' most sought-after amenity. Fashion etiquette suffered as women hurried from buildings without wearing hats. A visitor at the

Johnson Hotel attributed shaking walls to an overabundance of rats. An Academy of Music audience panicked when the balcony swayed back and forth. Crowds pushed and shoved as someone screamed, "The building is falling in." An entertainer on stage, who did not feel the quake, momentarily attributed the audience's rapid exit to an old joke he had just recited. The manager of another performer credited the earthquake to the loud applause his client received.

Bewildered sportsmen in saloons witnessed billiard balls move without assistance from the players. The tremor befuddled a customer consuming a drink at a Sheriff Street (East Fourth Street) bar. He exclaimed, "Great guns! Can it be possible that the single drink I took is going to do me up?" At least sixty people died at the earthquake's epicenter in Charleston, West Virginia.

Cleveland's next encounter with an earthquake occurred in 1895. Windows rattled, doors slammed, beds moved and chandeliers swung. For many, the early morning earthquake substituted for a more mundane alarm clock. Centered in Charleston, Missouri, twenty states felt the tremor.

In 1897, Cleveland experienced an earthquake centered in Virginia. For the first time, local scientists used a seismograph, located in the basement of a Western Reserve University building, to confirm the occurrence of a tremor. In 1925, Cleveland felt an earthquake centered in Quebec. As usual, guests quickly abandoned higher floors of hotels as the structures started swaying. Telephone operators deserted their switchboards, creating service interruptions. The earthquake resulted in minimal physical or property damage, although chickens escaped from a henhouse on East Ninety-fourth Street near Lake Erie. The quake may have injured the pride, if not the body, of Marion Brewater. Singing at a banquet in the downtown New Amsterdam Hotel, Miss Brewater appeared oblivious to the tremor as she concentrated on her musical tasks. When an entire set of guests abruptly left during her performance, she wondered how a few off-key notes could have sparked such a strong audience reaction.

Witnesses described a 1928 Cleveland earthquake as "three abrupt tremors." Windows in the Terminal Tower rattled, but no major damage resulted. A few scientists attributed the earthquake to an aerial bombing demonstration conducted at Camp Perry near Port Clinton. The feature event consisted of dropping three three-hundred-pound bombs during a timeframe matching the occurrence of the three tremors. The following year, Cleveland felt an earthquake centered about two hundred miles south of Buffalo. Just three months later, a major earthquake anchored under the Atlantic Ocean rocked the Atlantic coast from New York to Newfoundland.

Workers in the downtown Hanna Building endured thirty seconds of swaying chandeliers and rattling chairs.

In 1935, an estimated 6.25-magnitude earthquake, centered in Quebec, blasted three Canadian provinces and seventeen states. The earthquake reached Cleveland at 1:07 a.m. and lasted about thirty seconds. The *Plain Dealer* reported that the tremor "shook buildings as if they were poles." About one hundred guests at East Ninth Street's Hotel Gilsey gathered in the lobby to converse about the peculiar incident. The impromptu meeting continued until 2:00 a.m. as visitors discussed earthquakes and compared experiences.

Several small tremors developed in Cleveland during the first two months of 1937. A more severe earthquake, centered near Columbus, struck in early March. The Penton Building, in the Warehouse District, swayed for several seconds while doors and windows rattled. The next week, Cleveland recorded its fourth earthquake in two months. The biggest casualty of this earthquake, also centered in Columbus, may have been the demise of two cases of beer tumbling from an East Ninth Street restaurant shelf.

On January 31, 1986, Cleveland encountered an earthquake with a northeast Ohio epicenter located along a Lake County fault. A receptionist on the thirty-fifth floor of the National City Bank tower observed buildings swaying. When Severance Hall chandeliers started swinging, Cleveland Orchestra musicians halted their rehearsal in the middle of Dvorak's Seventh Symphony. In Columbus, bookshelves bounced up and down in the office of Michael Hansen, later the director of the Ohio Seismic Network.

Earthquake activity in northeast Ohio has not diminished in recent years. Scientists attribute the higher level of reported activity to a combination of greater awareness, more sophisticated measuring devices and implementation of procedures to continuously monitor ground motion in northeast Ohio.

Part II

INFAMOUS LAKE EFFECTS

THE SNOW MACHINE

In February 1972, the Eastern Snow Conference held its annual meeting in Oswego, New York, a town about thirty-five miles north of Syracuse. About one hundred scientists, engineers, professors, students and guests gathered to discuss snow-related issues. During the two-day conference, participants gained some unanticipated, firsthand knowledge regarding lake-effect snow. Fifty-six inches of snow dropped on their meeting place, completely isolating the attendees from the outside world and extending their visit several additional days. The conference did not return to Oswego for twenty years, and when it did, planners picked the first week of June to hold the meeting.

Lake-effect snow is a rare weather phenomenon existing in only a handful of locations on the entire planet. Although Cleveland is one of those special places, the five Great Lakes are all prolific generators of snow. Some of the resulting snowbelts make Cleveland winters almost seem akin to a tropical paradise. The hamlets of upstate New York's Tug Hill Plateau, immediately east of Lake Ontario, are too small to be classified as villages or towns. It's not difficult to understand why this region is so sparsely populated. In 1997, the hamlet of Montague endured 78 inches of snow in a twenty-four-hour period. During the winter of 1976–77, a snow accumulation of almost 467 inches descended on Hooker, another area hamlet. Lodges in the Tug Hill Plateau are sometimes built with an auxiliary front door placed directly

Although Lake Erie creates its share of havoc, the snow machine also produces beautifully picturesque settings, such as this 1931 scene in the Shakespearean cultural garden. *Courtesy of Special Collections, Michael Schwartz Library, Cleveland State University.*

above the ground-level entrance. The second-floor entry is used when the ground level cannot be accessed because of snowdrifts.

Lake Erie's snowbelt begins in northeast Ohio and continues into Pennsylvania and New York. The local portion of this snowbelt encompasses eastern Cuyahoga County, as well as Geauga, Lake and Ashtabula Counties.

In 1969, Christmas holiday shoppers on Euclid Avenue, near Public Square, endured a snowstorm. *Courtesy of Cleveland Public Library, Photograph Collection.*

Residents of Chardon, situated in Geauga County about thirty-five miles east of downtown Cleveland, expect more than one hundred inches in a typical winter. As if the primary snowbelt isn't enough, a secondary belt takes in southern Cuyahoga County, as well as Medina, Summit, Portage and northern Trumbull Counties.

Although any large lake in a cold climate is capable of producing lake-effect snow, very few bodies of water actually create sizeable snows. The process requires cold air to move across warmer water, drawing moisture upward as it cools to form snow clouds. A sufficiently large lake is needed to extract adequate moisture to create snow. The lake cannot be located too far to the north because, when a lake freezes, not enough moisture is drawn upward to form snow clouds. Since Lake Erie is shallow and prone to freezing, Cleveland is often spared lake-effect snow from mid-January to the end of February.

An effective snow machine needs a big assist from the topography of the nearby land. Elevations higher than the lake significantly increase the chance of lake-effect snow because the higher terrain causes air to rise to greater heights where cooler air forms snow at a rapid rate. Cleveland's eastern suburban "Heights" locale (the western end of the Appalachian foothills) is about 430 feet higher than Lake Erie. Even more extreme parts of Geauga County extend 1,680 feet above the lake. These higher elevations create the eastern snowbelt. In contrast, Cleveland's western suburbs consist of relatively flat land not much higher than the lake. In this region, little or no lake-effect snow is created since snow is deposited gradually over a large distance.

While characteristics of the lake and nearby land are vital in producing lake-effect snows, actual snowfall is amazingly unpredictable. During a 1962 snowstorm, not one flake of snow fell on Lake Erie's shoreline in Euclid, an eastern suburb of Cleveland. Yet an almost unbelievable nineteen inches accumulated a mere half mile to the south. Thus, more variables are required to explain the frequency and ferocity of lake-effect storms.

One important factor is the difference between the temperatures of the lake and air. A disparity of at least twenty degrees is required, while differences of more than fifty degrees are often aligned with very cold winds that are less likely to draw large amounts of water from the lake. The wind must pass across about fifty miles of a lake's surface before lake-effect snow develops. Generally, larger distances generate more snow. A minimum wind speed of eleven miles per hour is usually required to move air over the lake and onto the shore. But wind speeds of more than forty miles per hour may cause air to travel too quickly to absorb the needed heat and moisture.

Wind direction also influences the amount of time potential lake-effect snow remains over the lake. North winds across Lake Erie travel at most the 57-mile width of the lake before reaching Cleveland. But southwest winds can travel the entire 241-mile length of the lake, dumping substantially more snow on Buffalo.

A variable acting alone rarely causes a lake-effect snowstorm; the interaction of several factors is needed. In an extreme case, four of the Great Lakes once conspired with wind direction, wind distance and land elevation to create a massive storm. The wind moved across Lake Superior, down to Lake Huron, across parts of Lake Erie and over nearly all of Lake Ontario. A tremendous lake-effect snow arose when the wind finally reached the rising terrain of Mother Nature's much-maltreated Tug Hill Plateau.

In addition to keeping snowplowing companies in business, northeast Ohio's lake-effect snowstorms generate important positive contributions to the local environment. Snow cover prevents moisture loss in shrubs and

On snow-covered streets, even careful pedestrians experience an occasional tumble as witnessed by this 1982 fall on Superior Avenue at Public Square. *Courtesy of Cleveland Public Library, Photograph Collection.*

garden vegetation, resulting in healthier plants. Serving as a wind barrier, snow improves and prolongs the life of perennials, bulbs and ground cover. The snow's insulating effect enhances the flavor of locally produced wines. Snow replenishes underground water tables, protects soil against erosion

In 1984, paramedics tended to a victim from a snow-related multicar accident on a ramp to the Memorial Shoreway. *Courtesy of Cleveland Public Library, Photograph Collection.*

and increases the water level of the Great Lakes. Although not perfectly correlated with lake-effect snow, colder winters also enhance the flavor of carrots, celery, Brussels sprouts and parsnips.

JUDGMENT DAY ON LAKE ERIE

John Eberling and his younger brother, Edward, had invited Robert Michaels on a fishing expedition near Cleveland's west side Perkins Beach. As they cast their rods from a jetty in the early morning of May 31, 1942, a full moon and bright stars failed to shed enough light for the three to comprehend the impending disaster. A wall of water threw Robert from the pier. John dove into the lake and briefly clutched Robert before losing his grip as the powerful wave receded. The seventh-grader drowned in the turmoil, while the brothers survived by clinging to rocks near the water's edge.

At the same time, Wallace and Esther Allen had joined George Forrler and Evelyn, his fourteen-year-old daughter, in a fishing expedition on a Bay Village pier. As George taught Evelyn how to cast her rod, he suddenly shouted, "Get down, Evelyn. There is a big wave coming." The giant swell swept all four into the lake. Wallace rescued Evelyn, but the withdrawing

The wave of a terrifying Lake Erie seiche is the focus of this artistic interpretation. *Courtesy of the* Plain Dealer.

wave carried Esther and George to their deaths. Firemen attempted for an hour to revive Esther once she was recovered, but without success. Seven hours later, rescuers found George's lifeless body.

Fifty miles to the east, the wave capsized two small boats. Had Merrill F. Riley remained clinging to his overturned craft, he would have been saved by a nearby boater. But Riley drowned attempting to swim to shore. Meanwhile, Orlo Lenney; his wife, Esther; and Merle Edward Diehl all died when the wave upended their boat.

Against enormous odds, others along the Lake Erie shore survived the massive surge. On Ashtabula's Walnut Beach break wall, the upwelling hurled thirty-five people into the lake, while seven fishermen in Perry Township landed, injured but alive, in a nearby ravine. If the wave had occurred several hours earlier, hundreds would have perished as Clevelanders filled Lake Erie beaches on the previous hot, muggy evening.

Lake Erie seemed very peaceful just before the arrival of this incredible wave, peaking at a height of about twenty feet and stretching one hundred miles from Bay Village to the Pennsylvania border. A second wave, reaching a maximum height of eight feet, emerged about fifteen minutes later. Scientists ruled out an earthquake or tides as the cause of the horror. A terrified Geneva man, running as fast as his legs could carry him away from the lake, offered his explanation to highway patrol officers: "It's Judgment Day. I'm tellin' you, it's Judgment Day."

The deadly upsurge, mimicking a tidal wave, is a lake phenomenon known as a seiche, a French word meaning "to sway back and forth." Seemingly in defiance of nature, this wave can rise to terrifying heights, often in an otherwise calm body of water. Initially formed by a force (such as strong winds, changes in atmospheric pressure, earthquakes, landslides or hurricanes), a seiche develops as water is pushed to one side of a lake, only to create a powerful reverse flow as the force subsides. Traveling back and forth between opposite shores, the wave can continue for days after the original force has ended.

All five Great Lakes create seiches; shallow Lake Erie is known for wind-driven waves. The much larger and deeper Lake Superior is more prone to atmospheric-driven disturbances, where significant differences in barometric pressure on opposite shores are fairly common. Most waves, generating little interest or excitement, are less than a foot high. Larger waves may remain unseen if they occur in less populated areas or at times when few people are present. Another reason for their apparent obscurity is not as intuitive. Some waves develop completely underwater and are not detectable on the lake's surface. The underwater wave moves on the boundaries of layers of warm and cold water, often far from the surface of the lake.

Reports of large, unexpected waves date back to Lake Erie's early explorers; one traveler observed "sudden waves and swells" on the lake created by "some invisible agent." On the morning of June 23, 1882, an eight-foot seiche submerged the East Ninth Street pier. Its enormous force damaged or destroyed many boats and created a novel fishing experience for Clevelanders. Propelling hundreds of herring and pike ashore, the wave produced a choice selection of fish without the bother of using bait or fishing poles. A homeless person, the only known fatality, drowned while sleeping near the lake.

In 1944, four people died as a result of a seiche caused by changes in wind directions. Allan Dipple, a recent graduate of Iowa State College working in a Cleveland war plant, drowned on a Rocky River beach. Thirteen-year-old Donald Booth stood on the shore near Gordon Park as a twelve-foot wave washed him thirty feet into Lake Erie. Donald's brother rushed into the lake and carried him twenty feet toward the shore, but another wave tore them apart, sending Donald to his death. On private beaches a few blocks apart, Emlyn T. Lewis and Anna Brass, each enjoying the water while sitting in inner tubes, drowned as the wave struck an area east of Wildwood State Park.

In 1948, sweltering heat lured boaters to water, fishermen to piers and swimmers to beaches. As Clevelanders enjoyed the summer evening, a six- to twenty-foot wall of water struck an area beginning near Cleveland's Edgewater Park and extending fifteen miles into Lorain County. Despite the potential for incredible tragedies, not one person died as a result of the summer wave.

Researchers have observed that lakes known to create seiches also seem to provide sanctuaries for celebrated sea monsters. Scotland's Loch Ness is the supposed home of Nessie, while North America's Lake Champlain is claimed to harbor Champ. In British Columbia, Lake Okanagan allegedly shelters Ogopogo. And Lake Erie is the purported dwelling place of northwest Ohio's South Bay Bessie. Part of the monster mystery is easily explainable. An underwater seiche could briefly propel a large piece of debris (such as a log or tree trunk) into the air above the lake's surface. A startled onlooker might easily mistake the soaring object for a monster. Yet accounts of Bessie's sightings are far more extensive than merely observing a rising and falling object.

Over the years, the creature has been estimated to be anywhere from ten to sixty feet in length. Descriptions have cited dark skin, red eyes, brown or red spots, humps and fins. The first recorded sighting occurred in 1793, even before the founding of Cleveland. The monster, spotted by the captain of a sloop while shooting at ducks near Sandusky, reportedly measured about sixteen feet in length. An 1815 report described a long, snakelike beast. In 1817, a boat crew viewed a sixty-foot, copper-colored monster. That same year, two French settlers near Toledo encountered a monster on the beach, describing it as between twenty and thirty feet in length and shaped like a large sturgeon. An 1818 report described a sea serpent with its head and tail erect about thirty feet above of the water. The beast, spotted by many members of a boat's crew, journeyed within fifty-five yards of the surprised group.

In 1892, two fishermen described a monster as a twenty-five-foot, snakelike creature, black with brown spots, propelling itself through the water using several large fins or flippers located about five feet from its head. First seen swimming four miles from shore, the beast later appeared resting in a cove. Two months later, an entire ship's crew witnessed a large area of churning and foaming water. A "huge sea serpent" appeared, initially "fighting with an unseen foe." The creature, with "viciously sparkling" eyes and large fins, then relaxed, stretching its full length of about fifty feet. In 1896, on Crystal Beach near Fort Erie, four eyewitnesses spent forty-five minutes observing a thirty-foot creature with a dog-shaped head and a pointy tail.

In 1909, employees of both the Union Salt Company and the American Steel and Wire Corporation reported seeing a "long and willowy" grayish-green sea monster, ten feet in length, with red spots. The creature disappeared below the lake's surface near Addison Road, rumored to be headed directly toward Euclid Beach. In 1913, the *Plain Dealer*, distraught because no reports of sea serpents had been submitted by the end of June, lamented that Lake Erie's reputation as a "Great Lake" might be in danger. The newspaper suggested that readers submit descriptions of monsters they may have recently seen or thought they had seen. The newspaper further instructed its readers, "Do not let facts hamper you…No one will believe you anyway."

In 1931, three different persons reported seeing a thirty-foot sea serpent. One newsman suggested that Lake Erie rumrunners probably hired the monster to frighten lawmen. But on July 21, 1931, Clifford Wilson and Francis Cogenstose, two fishermen from Cincinnati, allegedly captured a monster, beating the poor beast into submission with an oar. The men placed the monster in a box six feet long, three feet wide and two feet deep. The tight confinement necessitated coiling the beast while it remained unconscious from the oar clubbing. The event generated national attention, including an account in the *New York Times* describing the creature as twenty feet long and twelve inches at its thickest point. The Cleveland Museum of Natural History eventually examined the beast and identified it as python rather than a mysterious beast.

The Lake Erie monster apparently took a long respite during the Depression, World War II and the 1950s. In the 1960s, sightings west of Cleveland reoccurred. A Sandusky fisherman spotted a cigar-shaped creature, while a boater near South Bass Island claimed that a beast ventured within six feet of him. A visitor on the Cedar Point Causeway described seeing a monster "so large that it could easily capsize a boat." Another account pegged a creature as resembling an exceptionally long, black alligator.

By the 1980s, the reputed monster, later named South Bay Bessie (possibly to honor the nearby Davis-Besse nuclear power plant), had developed into a tourist attraction. In 1990, a Port Clinton newspaper established a toll-free telephone number to report monster sightings, while the city of Huron was home to the National Live Capture and Control Center for the Lake Erie Monster. Local businesses pledged $102,700 in cash and prizes for the monster's capture. The offer apparently still stands; to secure the reward, the beast must be of an unidentified aquatic species, be at least thirty feet long and weigh at least one thousand pounds. Lloyd's of London has insured the city in case a payment is actually made.

In the early 1990s, two Huron firefighters, standing on a third-floor balcony, witnessed a thirty-foot monster. A charter boat captain and his wife reported a twenty-foot creature near Kelleys Island. A family observed a thirty-five-foot creature with a snakelike head near Cedar Point. While in a rowboat, a fisherman in Vermilion sighted a thirty-foot beast. By 1993, Bessie had made the cover of *Weekly World News*. A three-page special report described her as a two-hundred-ton Lake Erie sea serpent. She bore the blame for the sinking of a thirty-eight-foot sailboat.

In 1994, the Huron River housed a thirty-five-foot wood, plastic and metal sculpture of the lake beast. The supposed likeness of Bessie remained until 2004, when the property's new owner temporarily evicted the artificial monster. Public opinion prevailed, and the sculpture returned in 2005. The creature has also entered Cleveland's sports culture. During Shaquille O'Neal's brief tenure as a Cleveland Cavalier, a *Plain Dealer* account described him as "rearing up like the Lake Erie monster around the rim." Cleveland's latest entry in the American Hockey League bears the name Lake Erie Monsters.

RETURN OF THE MAYFLIES

Three or four times each year, downtown Cleveland resembles a scene from a bad horror flick. Millions of insects swarm on buildings, sidewalks and pedestrians. The bugs float into people's hair and attach themselves to clothing. Even speaking becomes hazardous to anyone who does not enjoy a cloud of insects in his mouth. The culprits are mayflies, invading the city in dense swarms sometimes exceeding ten miles in length and easily tracked on Doppler weather radar.

The mayfly, about one inch in length, has an elongated body and transparent wings located on the insect's back. *Courtesy of Dr. Kenneth Krieger, Heidelberg College.*

Scientists believe that mayflies have visited the land that would become northern Ohio for centuries, but a rapid growth spurt began when humans settled the region. The increase came about not because the insects enjoyed our ancestors' company but rather from increases in municipal sewage dumped into the lake that supplied mayflies with desirable nutrients. On June 6, 1855, the *Cleveland Leader* reported, "Yesterday our city was filled with swarms of insects of the gnat species. So thick were they at the foot of Water Street [West Ninth Street] that it was almost impossible to see or breathe. Where they came from we know not; but certainly they never appeared in such numbers in this city before."

A decade later, Cleveland held Canada responsible for the invading insects. In 1868, the *Cleveland Leader* noted, "Swarms of Canadian flies appeared in Cleveland yesterday. They seem very peaceable and seldom attempt to bite. They resemble a large mosquito in size. Their appearance may be welcomed, if they remain harmless, for old people say that such insects destroy malaria in the atmosphere and conduce materially to the healthiness of a place." Citizens near Lake Erie's south shore soon named the pests "Canadian soldiers"; on the northern side, Canadians called the insects "Yankee soldiers."

Newspapers and the general public referred to Canadian soldiers as a generic reference for mayflies, midges and other flying pests. The confusion is understandable; Ohio is home to at least 114 distinct species of seemingly similar airborne nuisances. Mayflies (also called June bugs, duns, fishflies and shadflies) and midges (additionally known as muffleheads and gnats, as well as by much less complimentary names) do not belong to the same family. Based on early descriptions, midges probably caused the 1855 and 1868 invasions. More recently, somewhere between 9 and 10 million midges attacked New York Yankee closer Joba Chamberlain during the 2007 baseball playoffs.

By 1915, Canadian soldiers were selling for fifty cents per hundred as an excellent bait, especially for luring blue gills. The insects' favorite landing places are white or reflective objects, such as fresh paint, clean windows and automobile windshields. In the 1920s, the pests landed on downtown store windows, obstructing shoppers' views of the latest fashions. By the 1950s, the insects had chosen Cleveland's new glass buildings as prime landing sites.

During the Depression, Sandusky used trucks to carry away large volumes of dead Canadian soldiers. As the decade progressed, the *Cleveland Press* became thoroughly disgusted with the insects. On July 1, 1936, the newspaper composed the following editorial titled "The Gandhi of Insects":

> *We may not care for flies, mosquitoes, wasps—bugs that bite and run—but at least they do run. We can have a certain respect for them as adversaries to catch and slap to death, if we are lucky. But Canadian Soldiers torment us with the fearsome weapon of passive resistance. They never hide, and they are perfectly willing to die—anywhere. It isn't even necessary to hit them—they land, swoon, and perish. At this season their corpses cover the shore, windshields of passing autos, the sides of tents and houses. Give us a bug that eats and runs, or stays to sting and fight it out.*

In 1939, downtown motorists complained that the insects hampered their vision, while pedestrians walking on sidewalks created a cracking noise similar to a popular breakfast cereal. In 1943, the *Cleveland Press* offered this warning: "MILITARY NOTICE: Canadian Soldiers Once Again Have Invaded Cleveland." Five years later, the *Press* reported, "Canadian Soldiers Land, Flock to Taverns." Since the insects do not drink, scientists speculated that the bright lights on the outside of the taverns may have attracted the bugs.

As the invasions continued, merchants on East Ninth Street used snow shovels to remove the insects from sidewalks. The evening of July 22, 1951,

In 1948, a night manager swept a harvest of Canadian soldiers from the sidewalk of a downtown Cleveland Royal Castle hamburger restaurant. *Courtesy of Special Collections, Michael Schwartz Library, Cleveland State University.*

In the 1940s, pedestrians walking on downtown Cleveland streets heard a crunching sound as they stepped on a portion of the millions of insects occupying the city's sidewalks. *Courtesy of Special Collections, Michael Schwartz Library, Cleveland State University.*

produced an especially large swarm in northwest Ohio. Biologists estimated that about 32.4 million mayflies congregated around just one lamppost in Middle Bass Island, less than fifty miles west of Cleveland. The density of mayflies on lawns in nearby Put-in-Bay rose to 2,650 per square foot. Two years later, the mayflies abruptly disappeared.

An extreme loss of oxygen in Lake Erie caused the insects' demise, but the reason for the oxygen loss is not known. One explanation places the blame on pollutants contaminating the sediment, in turn creating excessive algae growth. This thick green scum commonly occurred in Lake Erie during the 1950s. When the algae died and decayed, a layer may have formed containing no oxygen.

In 1994, a remarkable resurgence of the mayflies started west of Cleveland. Scientists and environmentalists hailed their return as marvelous news. Mayflies thrive in clean water, and their comeback offered evidence that the water quality of Lake Erie had improved. But their return also created its share of chaos. Masses of mayflies, settling on electric utility equipment, created power outages in Sandusky and Cedar Point. Large numbers of the dead insects accumulating on the lake's surface clogged and overheated pleasure boat engines. Today, motorists are warned that the squashing of huge numbers of mayflies may lead to slick roads.

The lifespan of the adult mayfly is about twenty-four hours. The insects cannot crawl, walk, bite, sting or even eat. As dusk arrives, mayflies mate in flight, after which the male dies immediately. The female flies back to the water; she drowns after depositing as many as eight thousand eggs. The eggs sink into sediment at the bottom of the lake. Larvae hatch after a period of two weeks to several months, feeding on the remains of plants, animals, algae and microorganisms. Nymphs rise to the lake's surface and molt into a subimago. After about one day, the subimago sheds its skin and becomes an adult, only to die in about one day. But mayflies remain a nuisance even in death. Swarms of the deceased insects develop a fish-like smell, while their decomposing bodies attract flies. A reasonable number of people living where mayflies mate develop seasonal hay fever and sometimes serious asthma.

Mayflies are a choice delicacy for walleye, smallmouth bass, channel catfish, freshwater drum and yellow and white perch. Yellow perch feed directly on the bottom-dwelling nymphs. Other fish eat the mayflies as they swim to the lake's surface after hatching. Dogs, cats and birds also enjoy dining on fresh mayflies. In fact, humans may be the only animal species not purposely consuming mayflies. Folk singer Alex Bevan is attempting to change humans' reluctance to consume the pesky creatures with his original composition "Mayfly Stew." He also tagged his 2006 concert appearances the Lord of the Mayflies Tour.

MAYFLY STEW
Composed by Alex Bevan

Settle back friends, take a sip or two
I've got a little recipe I'd like to share with you
It's been handed down for years on South Bass Island
It's tasty, it's delectable, it's really a fine one
You make it in the early part of summer time
From the freshest ingredients that you can find
It's not deep fried perch or walleye barbecue
It's genuine Put-in-Bay Mayfly stew

CHORUS: Mayfly stew, mayfly stew, pour me out another bowl or two
It's nutritious and delicious and it looks like glue
It's genuine Put-in-Bay mayfly stew!

Start with some Mayflies, I'd say about a million
Put them in the fridge so they can start chillin'
Soak them in water with a little bit of salt
A big "BAM" of essence and just a pinch of malt
Then you chop up some garlic—about a hundred and fifty cloves
Some onion, some celery, maybe a couple of tomatoes
To complete your preparation you'll need to make a stock
So go snag a carp from the public docks…Ahhh!
Put it in a pot, cover 'em with water
Bring it to a boil and I tell you, you nearly got 'er
Let 'er simmer down, pour in a beer
Then strain the liquid out until you've got it nice and clear

(Repeat chorus)

I should probably mention here the best way to catch 'em
Is you go down to the lake shore when they all start hatchin'
Wear a white shirt, take along a flashlight
And you should get your quota by the end of the night
If you're not a gourmet, then buddy you should just go

To De Riviera park when the sun gets kinda low
Take along a shovel, take along a fishing net
And you can get what you need without any sweat
Make sure you catch the young ones—don't take no oldies
They should have a tinge of green and not be brown or moldy
Their wings should be folded up and not in a bunch
And their abdomens should pop with a satisfying crunch

(Repeat chorus)

Take the Mayflies from the fridge and put them in a blender
Then push the puree button and let it spin until you render
Every little carcass into a uniform mass
And then get a spoon and take a little taste test
Add some cayenne and your preferential spice
(I find parsley, sage, rosemary and thyme work nice!)
And then mix it with the stock and reduce it 'til it thickens
Be sure to cook it slow and stir it like the dickens
It'll start to smell so good that it'll put you in a coma
Your friends and the police with stop to check out the aroma
So ladle 'em up a big dish, have a celebration
Put live ones on the top…that's your presentation

(Repeat chorus)

From Alex Bevan's The Life and Times of Sweetwater Pete. *Lyrics*
© 2004. Used with permission.

Part III

ASTOUNDING EXTREMES

THE YEAR WITHOUT A SUMMER

Back in 1816, Cleveland's one hundred or so inhabitants faced difficult times living in a near-wilderness. A massive volcanic eruption in far-off Indonesia or the sun's magnetic force reaching a cyclical low point probably did not cause avid dinner conversation among the hardworking settlers. But an especially memorable hometown blizzard must have attracted their attention. Three people reportedly froze to death in the brutal June storm. More snow followed in July. Erupting volcanoes, changes in the sun's force and summer blizzards amazingly combined to play a vital role in the future rapid development of Cleveland.

The civilized world has never witnessed, either before or since, an explosion as massive as the 1815 volcanic eruption on Tambora, a mountain on the Sumbawa Island in Indonesia. Only twenty-six of the island's twelve thousand inhabitants survived the blast. In total, about ninety thousand people perished either directly from the eruption or indirectly from an ensuing famine. By the following year, pollution had impeded the sun's ability to heat the Northern Hemisphere as Earth's atmosphere trapped two hundred megatons of dust, rock and aerosols. Four years earlier, Clevelanders had also endured a June snowfall, suggesting circumstances other than the volcano contributed to the cold 1816 summer. The conspiring factors included a relative low point in the sun's magnetic force, a long-term cyclical tilt in the planet's rotation and a recurring change in the shape of the planet's orbit around the sun.

On July 4, 1827, the first canalboat arrived in Cleveland, ushering in nearly a century of population growth. *Courtesy of Cleveland Public Library, Photograph Collection.*

In 1816, August frosts and snows destroyed New England crops, while sheep froze in meadows. And even more menacing circumstances threatened eastern farmers. Most of the fertile soil had already been appropriated. Severe rains had damaged or destroyed many mills along the rivers. The War of 1812 disrupted commerce, while a spotted fever epidemic plagued inhabitants. Facing complete ruin, New England residents accelerated a westward migration already in progress. The farmers knew that western states offered improved opportunities for growing crops and a perceived better life.

The cold summer provided the impetus to hasten westward journeys, in the process creating a need for better transportation. The migration led to the development of the Erie Canal and Ohio Canal, the latter opening in 1830 with Cleveland as the Lake Erie terminus.

In 1820, Cleveland's population amounted to only 606 hearty souls, with no apparent prospect for improvement. Jump-started by the cold 1816 summer, the canal turned into the catalyst for Cleveland's extraordinary growth. A century later, the former frontier village had propelled itself into the fifth-largest city in the United States. In addition to its economic impact, the canal also helped transform Cleveland from a New England village into a city teeming with immigrants. The first wave of immigration assisted in building the canal, while later newcomers found employment in the industries that the canal helped build.

THE PHANTOM ICE AGE

By 1978, the arrival of a new ice age appeared imminent. Throughout much of the United States and Europe, two extraordinarily cold back-to-back winters seemed to foretell a frigid future. Scientists had offered dire warnings about global cooling even before the bitter winters arrived. In 1975, the Central Intelligence Agency prophesized the arrival of a mini ice age, deeming the economic and political consequences "almost beyond comprehension." The National Academy of Scientists speculated that the transition to a colder climate had already begun. Some scientists viewed a ten-thousand-year ice age as a serious possibility, with cold weather eventually pushing glaciers back into the United States.

The media joined the global cooling bandwagon. Leading newspapers and popular magazines, including the *Saturday Evening Post, Newsweek* and *U.S. News and World Report*, featured articles about the anticipated climate disaster. A *Newsweek* article claimed that evidence supporting global cooling "has now begun to accumulate so massively that meteorologists are hard-pressed to keep up with it." *International Wildlife* announced that "the threat of a new ice age must now stand alongside nuclear war as a likely source of wholesale death and misery for mankind." Provocatively titled books, such as *The Weather Conspiracy: The Coming of the New Ice Age*, captured the interest of many readers. Carl Sagan, in his popular television series *Cosmos*, warned that catastrophic cooling could develop because of disappearing forests.

In 1970, two women battled harsh weather at the intersection of Snow and Pearl roads. A United Airlines advertisement suggested a more inviting alternative. *Courtesy of Cleveland Public Library, Photograph Collection.*

Clevelanders had no difficulty believing that colder weather had arrived. Except for the winter of 1962–63, the city had not experienced cold temperatures anywhere near the magnitude of the mid-1970s since the World War I era. In 1976, the bitter winter weather began in the fourth week of autumn. Ice-covered bridges caused dual fifteen-car accidents on both sides of Interstate 71 during the morning rush hour on October 27. The temperature tumbled to five degrees below zero on December 2, while Lake Erie's water temperature dropped to freezing on December 14, the earliest date on record for both events. On December 20, a major snowstorm dropped more than eight inches of snow on Cleveland and sixteen inches in the eastern snowbelt. The year concluded with a low temperature of eleven degrees below zero.

On January 9, 1977, a storm created "near blizzard" conditions as it dumped more than five inches of snow while blasting Cleveland with winds gusting to thirty miles per hour. Clevelanders waited only a short time for an official blizzard, which arrived on January 28. Beside the snow and wind, January turned into a blockbuster month for intense cold. Cleveland's temperature dropped below freezing at 10:00 p.m. on December 26 and never climbed back up to the freezing mark again until 8:30 a.m. on February 3. The high that day rose to only thirty-four degrees. The temperature remained below zero for a fifty-five-hour period beginning on January 16. With a low of seventeen degrees below zero, the high temperature on January 17 soared to two below zero.

Snow shoveling in January accounted for nineteen fatal heart attacks in Cleveland; exposure to the cold claimed five additional lives. Three elderly people froze to death in their homes. General Motors, Ford, General Electric, Republic Steel and Jones & Laughlin Steel furloughed thousands of workers as a depleted supply of natural gas limited manufacturing operations. On the positive side, homicides in Cleveland dropped 56 percent, and serious crime declined 16 percent when compared with the previous January. Although retail sales plunged, purchases of gloves, automobile batteries, antifreeze and furnace repair parts increased substantially. Of course, Cleveland weather still produced its peculiarities. A high of sixty-eight degrees tied the mark for the warmest ever February 23. As a parting shot, another snowstorm blasted northeast Ohio on April 6 as a foot of snow covered the eastern suburbs.

The winter of 1977–78 is best remembered for its frequent snowstorms. The snow began in earnest on November 11 when a foot of snow roared through the eastern suburbs, accompanied by thunder and lightning. Three major snowstorms blasted the city in December and January. The worst blizzard in the city's history followed the trio of tempests.

The first snowstorm arrived early in December. About three inches of snow and thirty- to forty-mile-per-hour winds reduced visibility to zero on December 6. Cleveland Hopkins Airport closed for fifteen hours. Six inches of new snow, with wind gusts of forty-eight miles per hour, greeted evening rush-hour travelers on December 8, extending the commute to well past 8:00 p.m. Downtown hotels filled quickly as more than 1,500 workers sought refuge. The Hotel Sterling, at East Thirtieth Street and Prospect Avenue, soon turned into the closest hotel with available rooms. The airport, canceling about one hundred departing flights, closed for the second time in three days. Snow shoveling took the lives of thirteen people in Cuyahoga County during the three-day storm.

On January 8, the second snowstorm delivered eight inches of snow and winds gusting to forty miles per hour. A RTA bus, on a ten-mile route from downtown to the Parmatown shopping mall, left Public Square at 3:30 p.m. and arrived at the mall at 11:00 p.m. Fifty riders of another RTA bus literally took matters into their own hands by pushing the bus out of a large snowdrift. A tow truck, dispatched to rescue a police car stranded in the snow, experienced the same fate during its failed mission. Twenty miles south of Cleveland, at the Richfield Coliseum, some of the 17,500 fans of the rock group KISS spent the night in dressing rooms and offices. A family choosing to drive home spent twelve hours on the road before reaching their Mentor destination. The Ohio National Guard searched northeast highways for stranded concert enthusiasts. Cleveland Hopkins Airport made a valiant but dangerous attempt to remain open during the storm. Ice and poor visibility combined to strand two planes in airport snowdrifts, while a snowplow sat trapped on a runway. Eventually, the entire airport shut down again.

The third major snowstorm attacked Cleveland on January 20. Two people died of heart attacks while shoveling snow. A snowplow struck another person. Ten inches of snow delayed the grand opening of the Interstate 480 link between Garfield Heights and Interstate 77. And the airport closed again. At this point, the monthly snow accumulation of 30.6 inches surpassed the old snowfall record of 28.0 inches set in 1910. But the worst weather, the great blizzard of 1978, had not yet arrived.

The much-heralded ice age never materialized. The cooling cycle had actually started in the mid-1940s, reached its peak in the mid-1970s and reversed itself in the 1980s.

PRAYING FOR RAIN

Hot weather is no stranger to Cleveland. Moses Cleaveland's original surveying party reported suffering from "intense heat and a humid atmosphere." Three especially severe droughts developed during the middle of the nineteenth century. Temperatures during an 1845 drought supposedly ranged from 100 to 120 degrees in the sun; four people died in the suffocating heat. According to the *Cleveland Leader*, farmers faced the inevitable crop loss with a combination of determination, courage and faith: "Ohio farmers are not the men to give way to despondency. They have too much confidence in Providence and their fertile soil for that."

On June 25, 1852, the *Daily True Democratic* reported, "For more than a week past, all hereabouts have been praying for rain to lay this horrible dust." Two months later, on August 18, the newspaper noted, "We are sadly in need of rain. Our farmers complain that unless we have some soon, everything will dry up." Seven years later, July temperatures exceeded one hundred degrees. The *Cleveland Leader* offered some practical advice: "Hot weather prompts the suggestion of water as an effective cooling agent. We highly recommend the use of bath tubs."

A remarkable 1934 western dust storm traveled across the country before dissipating in the Atlantic Ocean. The storm passed through Cleveland on its lengthy journey. *Courtesy of Cleveland Public Library, Photograph Collection.*

In the twentieth century, Cleveland and a vast portion of the United States struggled through two especially severe periods of dry weather. A 1934 drought, engulfing more than 75 percent of the country, triggered an incredible dust storm. Strong winds grabbed 350 million tons of earth in Montana and Wyoming, propelling it eastward toward the Atlantic Ocean. Along its route, the dust cloud, measuring 1,500 miles in length and 900 miles in width, dropped 12 million pounds of dust on Chicago. On May 10, the tempest reached Cleveland, creating an unusual green-tinted morning sunrise. The mammoth dust storm continued east, depositing earth on ships 300 miles offshore in the Atlantic Ocean. The summer remained hot even after the dust storm. On July 24, the temperature in Cleveland reached ninety-nine degrees. Sunstroke killed a farmer pitching hay in Middleburgh Heights. Thousands of Clevelanders, escaping the heat of their homes, slept in public parks that night. Extra police patrolled the areas to provide safety for the sleeping citizens.

In 1988, Cleveland suffered through another prolonged drought. Little rain fell during April and May. In June, lack of rain combined with five all-time daily high temperatures. Priests and ministers prayed for rain during Sunday services. Leaders in Clyde, Ohio, developed a very proactive stance; a Sioux Indian, imported from South Dakota, collected $2,000 to perform an ancient pipe-smoking ceremony. About 4,500 curious citizens attended the ritual designed to restore harmony in nature and create lightning, thunder and rain within four days. Despite the prayers and pipes, not a drop of rain fell that week.

Cleveland's temperatures continued to climb. The June 25 reading of 104 degrees is still the hottest ever officially recorded in the city. Three days later, the Cleveland temperature declined to a record-breaking June low of 49 degrees. Another daily record fell on June 30 when the thermometer dropped to 48 degrees. But temperatures warmed again, and little rain fell.

As the drought continued, Ohio's agricultural output deteriorated. Soybeans, the state's top cash crop, did not suffer a negative impact, but the harvest of corn, Ohio's second-largest crop, declined 41 percent from the previous year. Revenue information regarding the state's third-largest crop is not as precise. In 1987, sale of marijuana constituted an approximate $540 million business. Meigs County, in the southern part of the state, enjoyed a national reputation for supplying one of the country's best crops, with prime pot selling for between $2,000 and $3,000 per pound. But dealers observed a sharp reduction in availability as the drought progressed. On the other hand, because turkeys mature best in drier climates, Ohio produced its finest Thanksgiving turkey crop in years. Cleveland's drought ended abruptly as September ushered in normal temperatures and a generous supply of rain.

TROUBLED WATER

The tragic aftermath of an August 24, 1975 thunderstorm and subsequent flood seems almost implausible. Lightning struck and killed two twelve-year-old Cleveland Heights boys just finishing football practice. A nine-year-old girl, wading through water on West 130th Street, fell through an open manhole. She drowned as the water hurled her two miles through the Cleveland sewer system. A swift current overtook and killed a man swimming on Sterns Road as he attempted to help his daughter locate an automobile she had abandoned in the storm. A husband and wife on East 97th Street squeezed into a two-foot-wide crawl space to avoid drowning as water continued to rise in their home. A neighbor freed the couple by cutting a hole in the wall after removing aluminum siding from the home. As an automobile ran into floodwaters at West 130th Street and Puritas Road, a

A 1975 flood claimed the lives of several Clevelanders, including a man who drowned on Stearns Road attempting to help his daughter locate her abandoned automobile. *Courtesy of Special Collections, Michael Schwartz Library, Cleveland State University.*

seventy-seven-year-old woman pushed her eighty-three-year-old husband out of the car window, saving his life. She also survived the ordeal.

One of nature's most destructive forces, flooding has a long history of devastation and death in the Cleveland area. In 1822, three days of continuous rain created a torrent that swept away a Tinker's Creek sawmill. Six years later, water consumed several passengers when a stagecoach driver attempted to cross the rain-swelled Rocky River. In 1839, the same flooded river carried a canoe rider to his death; the victim left a widow and eight children.

In 1901, a heavy ten-hour rain washed away ground beneath streetcar tracks, leaving them suspended in air. Houses floated from their foundations; two East Eighty-ninth Street homes collapsed at the same time, barely missing each other as they fell. But this storm is most remembered because of the gruesome sights occurring at St. Joseph and St. John Cemeteries, located across from each other at Woodland Avenue and East Seventy-ninth Street. The bank of a brook running along St. Joseph Cemetery collapsed; the resulting deluge swept away headstones and caskets from both graveyards. The torrents ripped open coffins and hurled bones of decayed bodies through the running water, in the process attracting hundreds of inquisitive onlookers. A few miles away, in the Broadway neighborhood at an old cemetery that had been relocated in the 1870s, the flood unearthed a skull and bones from the earlier graveyard.

The great deluge of March 1913 constitutes the greatest natural disaster in Ohio's history, with a confirmed death toll of 467. Heavy rain in January soaked Ohio's soil. The waterlogged terrain froze as temperatures plunged in February and then thawed as March highs rose into the seventies. The continuous rain, melting snow and waterlogged ground created enormous flooding across the state. In Cleveland, the canal and Cuyahoga River merged to generate a raging torrent. The canalboat home of Charles Stebbins, torn from its moorings, raced downstream in the surging water until a neighbor in a rowboat and a canalboat operator combined to dramatically rescue the houseboat. The Chagrin River expanded from its normal width of one hundred feet to between one thousand and three thousand feet. Yet Cleveland escaped the horrors and death that developed throughout most of the state.

On January 19, 1959, a thirty-five-mile-per-hour wind created gusts of snow. The snow changed to rain, later freezing as night temperatures plunged to twelve degrees. When the temperature climbed to fifty degrees the next day, the *Plain Dealer* remarked, "Like a crafty baseball pitcher, winter served up a bewildering variety of offerings." The day following the newspaper's baseball

In 1937, floodwaters stalled traffic on Miles Avenue near East Ninety-third Street. *Courtesy of Special Collections, Michael Schwartz Library, Cleveland State University.*

In 1948, the swollen Chagrin River washed a four-room cottage down the river, into Lake Erie and onto the shore more than one mile from the river's mouth. *Courtesy of Cleveland Public Library, Photograph Collection.*

Normally less than five feet wide, Big Creek raged through the Roseland Golf Course on Tiedeman Road during a severe 1954 rainstorm. *Courtesy of Special Collections, Michael Schwartz Library, Cleveland State University.*

analogy, the heaviest January rain in northeast Ohio history blasted the area. Steady winds of sixty miles per hour, occasionally gusting to eighty miles per hour, accompanied the precipitation. The temperature, registering sixty degrees at 8:58 p.m., plunged to thirty-eight degrees in one hour.

Seven people in Greater Cleveland died that day. An accident on the raging Chagrin River claimed five lives. A boat overturned after hitting a tree just ten feet into a rescue mission. A husband, wife and mother, all wearing life jackets, drowned, along with two of the three rescue workers. Unable to reach the victims, witnesses watched the five cling to trees and listened to their pleas for help. Large chunks of ice, flying down the river, pounded each of the victims, causing all five to lose their grip and perish in the freezing water.

Unrelated accidents claimed two lives in Valley View. A truck driver died when he missed a turn and plunged into the Cuyahoga River. Floodwaters washed away an army private from an overturned truck during a rescue mission. Neighbors used a rowboat to successfully transport an expectant mother in labor out of Valley View and into a nearby hospital. The Big Creek overflowed into the Cleveland Zoo's lion house, flooding the building's

In the 1959 spring flood, water covered Route 21 in Cuyahoga Heights near Grant Avenue. *Courtesy of Special Collections, Michael Schwartz Library, Cleveland State University.*

In 1968, the ice-laden Chagrin River overflowed its banks, flooding nearby streets with both water and ice. *Courtesy of Cleveland Public Library, Photograph Collection.*

A 1972 rainstorm caused the normally docile Doan Creek to overflow onto Liberty Boulevard near East Eighty-eighth Street. *Courtesy of Special Collections, Michael Schwartz Library, Cleveland State University.*

basement containing a reptile collection. The zoo reported that 165 of the 167 reptiles had drowned; even though all of the reptiles could swim, the completely flooded area shut off the air needed to breathe. Two days later, the zoo discovered that four rattlesnakes and a water moccasin had miraculously survived.

On January 30, 1968, heavy rains and ice-jammed rivers created severe flooding conditions to the east (Chagrin River) and west (Vermilion River) of Cleveland. In Vermilion, rats scampered from break walls as the river continued to rise. Thick ice needed to be removed from both rivers to alleviate flooding problems. The Chagrin River required detonating 1,800 sticks of dynamite to free water from the nearly one-foot-thick ice.

On August 2, 2007, hail and sixty-mile-per-hour wind gusts accompanied a freak rainstorm centered directly on downtown Cleveland. The ninety-minute storm, beginning at 3:20 p.m., disrupted rush-hour traffic and soaked fans leaving an afternoon baseball game. Burke Lakefront Airport reported an almost unbelievable 4.75 inches of rain during the short outburst. Adding to the strangeness of Cleveland weather, the National Weather Service, located less than ten miles from downtown, recorded not one drop of precipitation the entire day.

Part IV

CUYAHOGA RIVER TALES

A RAGING RIVER

Thirty cannon shells successfully smashed an 1881 rain-swollen ice jam on the Cuyahoga River. The ice threatened to create a massive flood by impeding torrents of rainwater from flowing down the river. Two years later, a steady rain, combined with melting ice and snow, shaped a spring flood extending three miles inland from the mouth of the river. The floodwaters reached three-quarters of a mile in width. Meanwhile, water rushing down Kingsbury Run merged with leaking oil from a Standard Oil plant east of the Flats. The flowing oil reached a boiler room at the Great Western Oil Works, where it ignited five thousand barrels of crude petroleum from a storage tank. The flowing inferno then caused a blaze at the paraffin works of the Meriam & Morgan Company. Reaching the Cuyahoga River, the burning oil continued to the main Standard Oil plant, where ten tanks holding about fifty thousand barrels of oil exploded. The fire burned for two days while the Industrial Valley remained submerged under water. In total, seven people died from the strange blend of fire and flooding.

In 1893, seventy hours of continuous rain caused the Cuyahoga River to reach its then-highest point on record. Uprooted trees, floating down the river, formed a dam to heighten the crisis. Flooding reached the second floor of homes along the river, while horses drowned in nearby pastures that floodwaters had transformed into lakes. A man drowned attempting to cross the river on a log. A lifesaving boat capsized, killing seven of the eight crew members in an attempt to rescue two men.

The flood propelled an entire lumberyard into Lake Erie. Pilferers used ropes and hooks to steal lumber floating down the river. When the task became too difficult, the thieves brought in wheelbarrows to remove whatever lumber remained in the yard. A fight broke out regarding the proper allocation of roofing shingles acquired by two robbers. Eventually, the men threw the shingles back into the river and adjourned to a saloon to continue discussing how the lost shingles should have been divided. Despite the severity of the flood, a tavern near Columbus Street served drinks while water flowed through the windows. At closing time, the proprietor departed in a boat.

In 1904, two days of rain caused a large mass of ice, flowing down the river, to jam near the Grasselli Chemical Company. A huge flood developed as an embankment between the river and canal gave way. The Flats resembled a half-mile-wide lake. Water submerged one mile of Wheeling & Lake Erie railroad, destroyed the Nickel Plate Railroad Bridge and reached levels of six feet in many buildings.

The highlight of this flood involved a bizarre sequence of events among three large ore carriers docked on the Cuyahoga River. The powerful water flow caused the *William E. Rees* to break its moorings. The flood hurled the ship, without a crew, down the Cuyahoga River, and it crashed into the *John W. Moore*. The impact of the collision liberated the *Moore*, which then joined the *Rees* on its flight downriver. Both ships then smashed into the *James B. Eads*, freeing it from its moorings. Side by side, the trio raced toward the Center Street Bridge. Amazingly, all three cleared the bridge, but the *Moore* hit the *Eads* a second time, throwing it diagonally across the river. The impact caused the *Eads* to collide with both the Superior Viaduct and the B&O Railroad Bridge. The *Moore* also crashed into the Superior Viaduct, while the *Rees* trapped itself in a small space between the other two ships. Tightly jammed together, the three ships completely blocked the river for several days.

Despite the Cuyahoga River's long history of flooding, the 1913 torrent stands in a class by itself. The river washed away docks and lumberyards and drove scores of families from their homes while trapping others inside their houses. A six-foot-high wall of water drove occupants to upper floors of private homes and rooming houses below the Harvard-Denison Bridge. The rapid flow of the river hindered rescue rowboats and rafts as tops of boxcars and roofs of houses rushed down the river at speeds of up to twenty miles per hour.

The water's force pushed part of the West Third Street Bridge 150 feet from its turntable. The storm ripped the freighter *William Henry Mack* from its moorings. Wintering in the Cuyahoga River, the ship crashed into and destroyed the bridge. The tugboat *Grace*, torn from its docking, just missed hitting the *Mack*. The *Charles Beatty*, a lumber boat, and the *Caldeer*, an industrial vessel, sailed down the river unattended. The tugboat *James Burns* broke loose with its crew aboard and roared into Lake Erie.

While the river raged, eleven people sought refuge on the roof of a building, while twenty-three others huddled on the top of a freight car. Fire broke out in a lumberyard already filling with water. Firefighters, unable to reach the building with their trucks, carried hoses in waist-high water. Patrons of a saloon discovered that floodwaters had cut off their only escape to higher floors. First acquiring shelter by climbing on the bar, they eventually ascended even higher to the top of an icebox. Rescuers cut a hole in the floor above and dropped a ladder to facilitate the customers' exit.

An engineer on a B&O freight train pulled the brakes after hearing a loud crash—the sound of a collapsing railroad bridge near Brookside Park. The train stopped three feet short of plunging into the deep gorge. Creeks and streams, normally small and unnoticed, overflowed their banks in Collinwood, flooding hundreds of factories, businesses and homes. Police moved to the second floor of their station when water rose to seven feet on the ground floor. A three-foot-deep stream roared down Saranac Road, where water accumulated to a level of nine feet at the intersection of East 152nd Street.

Both enterprising and dishonest citizens capitalized on the city's misery. For a fee, a boy offered to transport people around Collinwood in a rowboat. On the west side, a youth used a pony to establish a ferry service across flooded Clifton Boulevard. The *Cleveland News* warned readers of several women soliciting money for food relief in the name of the newspaper, although the *News* had not employed any collectors.

The floods ended commercial use of the Ohio Canal. Railroads had already rendered the canal obsolete, but many locks remained intact across the state. Dynamite purposefully destroyed some locks, allowing the flooding water to flow unimpeded. Damages from the flood, combined with the dynamiting, rendered the antiquated canal infrastructure of no practical value.

The 1913 flood inspired discussions about reducing the impact of future rains by widening the river at its mouth, as well as straightening and deepening the waterway. Although Congress provided funds for a preliminary study to identify the best approaches, a combination of legal, political and fundraising battles inhibited progress; in fact, Cleveland never even used the initial grant from Congress. During the Depression, the city received funds from the federal government to start and finish the task, although the justification had shifted to enhancing Cleveland's commercial interests rather than inhibiting floods. Although river flooding in the downtown area has been eliminated, portions of the river south of downtown continue to flood with any significant rainfall.

FLAMES ON THE CUYAHOGA RIVER

On June 22, 1969, a patch of the Cuyahoga River below a railroad bridge burst into flames. Sparks from a train traveling on the bridge probably started the fire. Reaching a height of five stories, the blaze damaged two railroad bridges before being brought under control. From beginning to end, the blaze lasted twenty-six minutes. No known pictures of the fire exist. The small number of actual witnesses believed that floating debris, rather than the water itself, caused the flames. The event generated little initial interest in Cleveland but eventually captured the imagination of the entire nation.

Two months after the fire, *Time* magazine published a story about the river burning, characterizing the Cuyahoga as not fit for "leaches and sludge worms that usually thrive on wastes." A sensational picture of the blazing Cuyahoga River accompanied the article. Carol Browner, the Environmental Protection Agency Administrator, dramatically depicted her recollection of the event: "I will never forget a photograph of flames, fire, shooting right out of the water in downtown Cleveland. It was the summer of 1969 and the Cuyahoga River was burning." But Browner had not viewed a photograph from the summer of 1969. With no available visuals, *Time* published a stock picture of a far more dramatic 1952 Cuyahoga River fire. The *New York Times* and *National Geographic* followed with their interpretations of the blazing river saga. Johnny Carson and other television entertainers joked about a city allowing its river to burn. The unfavorable publicity culminated with "Burn On," Randy Newman's ode to the fiery river.

Prior to the fire, Cleveland had already started a serious river-cleansing initiative. The city's voters approved a costly $100 million bond issue to finance cleanup of the Cuyahoga River while, at the same time, the federal government earmarked only $160 million for cleaning the entire nation's

In 1850, although the banks of the Cuyahoga River attracted commercial businesses, industry had not yet contaminated the water. *Courtesy of Cleveland Public Library, Photograph Collection.*

rivers. Cleveland received the unfavorable publicity, but the city held no monopoly on abuse of waterways. Fires have plagued the Passaic River in New Jersey, the Buffalo River in New York, the Rouge River in Michigan, the river leading into the Baltimore Harbor and the Houston Ship Channel. Although industrial pollution greatly escalated the process, for thousands of years waterways have been ignited by lightning and oil rising naturally to the tops of creeks and streams. In the 1700s, George Washington spoke of springs "luminous and inflammable by nature."

The first recorded fire on the Cuyahoga River took place on August 29, 1868. A spark from a tugboat's smokestack ignited oil that burned a wide section of the river near the West Third Street Bridge. Although gravely in danger, businesses on the riverbanks escaped extensive damage. A *Plain Dealer* editorial, discussing the polluted river, called on Cleveland to "rid the river of this nuisance at once." But conditions only worsened as the years passed. Rensselaer R. Herrick, mayor of Cleveland in 1881, referred to the Cuyahoga River as "an open sewer through the center of the city."

By this time, the area bordering the Cuyahoga River ranked high among the world's heaviest concentrations of industry. The twisting and turning river created numerous peninsulas, ideal space for industrial development. Many citizens viewed pollution as a sign of industrial strength—a tolerable side effect of progress. John D. Rockefeller, recalling the disposition of unwanted byproducts in the early days of oil refining, told a biographer, "Thousands and hundreds of thousands of barrels of it floated down the creeks and rivers, and the ground was saturated with it."

In 1887, a grain elevator fire set the river in flames. Three years later, the city council passed an ordinance against polluting rivers, although the protection centered on commercial issues rather than environmental concerns. The law prohibited river dumping that would "impede or obstruct navigation." Pollution seemed to be acceptable as long as the river remained clear for commerce. The 1890s drew to a close with an oil slick bursting into flames on December 31, 1899.

In 1912, workers loaded a Standard Oil barge with about 1 million gallons of gasoline from the company's refinery. Gasoline leaked into the river when the barge developed a breach in one of its seams. A spark from a passing tugboat most likely ignited a series of six explosions, but the cause might have been a match, a cigarette or a cigar thrown from the Jefferson Avenue Bridge. A three-hundred-yard section of the river exploded in flames. Although the barge did not blow up, the river still turned into a fiery holocaust.

A blue flame erupted from the water beneath workers caulking a scow on a dry dock across from the Standard Oil barge. Five men, toiling in a very confined space, had no chance to escape. Gas most likely paralyzed them before flames burned their bodies beyond recognition. Several other employees narrowly escaped the inferno. One worker, situated at the extreme end of the dry dock, leaped through flames and over burning docks. Another employee, suffering from an earlier injury, had planned to return to his job on the day of the fire. As he dressed to leave for work, his wife convinced him to rest his injury for one more day. A tugboat operator summarized his appraisal of working conditions on the Cuyahoga River with the remark, "We don't know at what moment the river is going to blaze up and destroy us."

In the 1930s, the Cuyahoga River continued its disgraceful existence. Oil, logs, timbers from rotted docks, broken hulls, oil-soaked pilings and other floating debris caused the river's temperature to sometimes exceed 110 degrees. Flammable methane bubbles created a constant risk of being ignited. In 1930, fire destroyed a Cleveland Grain Company elevator near the river. As fermented grain seeped into the river, the combination of oil and alcohol provided a new source of combustion. A month later, a strong wind blew sparks from the still-smoldering elevator into the Cuyahoga River. Huge flames rising from the river created menacing black clouds.

The river's condition deteriorated so badly that industry took the lead in calling attention to the problem. In 1936, a paper manufacturer objected to the city's practice of dumping raw sewage into the Kingsbury Run stream feeding the Cuyahoga River. In a resulting lawsuit, the city pleaded that it had used the stream as an open sewer since 1860, thus establishing a "prescriptive right" to continue such use. The court wholeheartedly agreed; in fact, the seventy-six years of pollution far exceeded the minimum twenty-one-year requirement necessary to keep the raw sewage flowing.

The river ignited again in 1941 and 1948. The latter fire's flames, peaking at more than one hundred feet, threatened to destroy the Clark Avenue Bridge. The river flared up again in 1949. This fire, spreading rapidly over floating oil scum, destroyed a railroad trestle and damaged Republic Steel's loading dock and pump house. The *Cleveland Press*, demanding immediate reform, didn't advocate ending the pollution. Instead, the newspaper recommended

The media used pictures from this serious 1952 Cuyahoga River fire in conjunction with stories about a much less spectacular 1969 blaze. *Courtesy of Cleveland Public Library, Photograph Collection.*

The 1952 fire threatened Standard Oil's refinery, but firefighters brought the blaze under control before it created a major catastrophe. *Courtesy of Cleveland Public Library, Photograph Collection.*

Cleveland's fire department should purchase and operate an oil skimmer so future messes could be efficiently cleaned before encountering a fire. Two years later, the river flared up again.

In May 1952, Fire Warden Bernard W. Mulcahy predicted, "The Cuyahoga River will burn." In September, he designated the river as "Cleveland's greatest fire hazard," envisioning the most dangerous place as "where Kingsbury Run empties into a slip adjacent to the Great Lakes Towing Company and the Standard Oil Company." Pictures of the site where Mulcahy predicted the fire showed six inches of oil covering the river. On November 1, 1952, an inferno started exactly where Mulcahy pinpointed the potential danger. The blaze destroyed three tugboats and most of the buildings in the Great Lakes Towing Company's repair yard. Spreading inland, the flames threatened Standard Oil's giant Number 1 Refinery. *Time* magazine used a picture from this blaze to accompany its coverage of the much less extensive 1969 fire.

In 1956, just four years after a river fire seriously endangered the downtown area, the Cuyahoga River erupted again. *Courtesy of Cleveland Public Library, Photograph Collection.*

The deplorable condition of the river at the Jefferson Avenue Bridge site illustrates early difficulties associated with assigning responsibility for the river pollution. Standard Oil received the majority of the negative publicity. Mulcahy suggested that the company's executives should be arrested. But a chemical analysis indicated that 85 percent of the oil at that point had actually entered the river from the Kingsbury Run stream before the river had reached the Standard Oil facility.

In 1951, the State of Ohio enacted legislation to control water pollution. Although the law prohibited the discharge of harmful substances without a valid permit issued by the state, Ohio freely granted permits to industrial users along the Cuyahoga River. Since the state law superseded any local laws, cities had no power to regulate any business obtaining a state permit. Carl Stokes, Cleveland's mayor at the time of the 1969 fire, claimed that the state had given industries the legal authority to pollute the Cuyahoga River. The state responded by claiming that the city's sewer system created river pollution and that Ohio might enact enforcement actions against the city.

Nearly all forms of desirable life had long since ceased to exist in this portion of the river. But the disappearance could not be blamed on any loss of interest on the part of fish. In October 1959, after an absence of decades, the river witnessed a remarkable short-term return of baby catfish, carp, minnows and shiners. The shutdown of all steel manufacturing during a prolonged labor strike from June 15 through November 7 provided the opportunity for the temporary visit. Given a fighting chance to survive, the fish seemed willing to reconcile with the Cuyahoga River. Not unexpectedly, the fish disappeared again when steel manufacturing resumed.

The condition of the Cuyahoga River improved substantially after the 1969 fire. Governmental agencies sponsored construction of sewer interceptors and wastewater-treatment plants and implementation of stronger pollution-control measures. In 1972, biologists found no fish in the Cuyahoga River between Cleveland and Akron. Thirty years later, sixty-two different species inhabited the same area. The fish, in turn, attracted bald eagles, great blue herons and a variety of animals.

As time passed, much of the nation tended to forgive, forget or ignore Cleveland's famous fire. Twenty-five years after the blaze, one national poll indicated that more people thought the 1969 river incident occurred in Pittsburgh. But in Cleveland, the burning Cuyahoga River continues to enliven local pop culture. In 2001, an initial Burning River Festival developed into an annual event in downtown Cleveland. The celebration promotes environmental education, along with offering live music and food from area restaurants. Vendors' cash registers are powered by solar panels, while a generator, running on vegetable oil, chills the food. The Burning River Foundation is dedicated to improving freshwater resources in northeast Ohio. Music lovers have enjoyed concerts by the Burning River Brass, Burning River Band, Burning River Ramblers and Pirates of the Burning River. A Cleveland entry in a roller derby league named themselves the Burning River Roller Girls. The Burning River Lacrosse organization helps promote the sport. The Burning River Developers is a professional group of software designers. Northeast Ohio is home to Burning River Glass, *Burning River Press*, Burning River Rentals (a real estate company), Burning River Boxer (breeders of boxer dogs) and Burning River Films (a fledging film company), while train enthusiasts enjoy the Burning River Model Railroad Club.

Part V

FIREFIGHTING SAGAS

DISTURBING BEHAVIOR

Back in 1811, village leaders first addressed Cleveland's firefighting needs by placing two buckets beside an eight-foot-wide public well on West Sixth Street near Superior Avenue. Developing no strategy for preventing or extinguishing fires, the town merely made the water available; each citizen assumed personal responsibility for his or her own fire protection. This seemingly archaic approach worked for seven years, largely because no serious fire took place.

Cleveland's fire fortunes soon changed for the worse. On March 9, 1819, the town recorded its first serious fire—a frame residential house in the Flats burned to the ground. Less than two months later, a blaze damaged a store on Superior Avenue. Village leaders ordered citizens to acquire a "good leather fire bucket." Failure to follow the edict resulted in continuing monthly fines of between five and fifteen dollars. Citizens faced a steeper fifty-dollar penalty for not "well securing" fires after 9:00 p.m. In contrast, Clevelanders allowing their geese to wander through the city incurred fines of only fifty cents.

In 1829, as the population of Cleveland passed the one thousand mark, town leaders spent $285 to acquire the city's first fire engine, a secondhand piece of equipment. This safety precaution turned into a serious political blunder. Citizens defeated the reelection of every trustee who voted for the purchase. Heeding public opinion, a new set of trustees promptly repudiated the fire engine contract.

Taken about the time of the Civil War, this photograph depicts one of Cleveland's last boisterous volunteer firefighting companies. *Courtesy of Cleveland Public Library, Photograph Collection.*

In 1830, a group of merchants, businessmen and lawyers created an unofficial firefighting organization. Three years later, the Live Oaks Fire Company No. 1, consisting of forty-five citizens, became the first formal volunteer firefighting association. Cleveland spent $700 to purchase a hand-pumping engine and built a firefighting headquarters at the Superior Hill, just west of West Ninth Street. When a fire alarm needed to be sounded, city resident Nicholas Quackenbush rang the Trinity Church tower bells (located at the southeast corner of St. Clair Avenue and West Third Street). Upon hearing the alarm, volunteers raced from their homes or places of employment to the engine houses, where the firefighters assembled before proceeding to the fire.

Horse-drawn or steam engines did not exist in the volunteer era; the volunteers used ropes to manually drag three-ton fire engines across rut-filled streets, up steep hills and through sand and mud. Concurrently, hose companies brought fire hose, connecting it to water supplies and fire engines. Sources for water included the canal, the Cuyahoga River or four cisterns located on street corners, although these cisterns often needed repair or lacked water.

In 1834, momentum to provide improved fire protection continued as Cleveland established a complete, integrated volunteer fire department.

A typical volunteer company included professionals, merchants, white-collar workers and both skilled and working-class laborers. A payment of $1 for each of eight annual drill meetings constituted their only monetary compensation. The chief received a salary of $150 per year but traditionally spent the money to purchase prizes for an annual dinner and ball.

In 1835, a disastrous fire obliterated three complete business blocks, destroying twenty-two stores and offices. The blaze, originating in the kitchen of a boardinghouse, caused Cleveland's first fatality attributed to fire. Louisa Rider, a servant, burned to death as she attempted to flee from the conflagration. As usual, the fire produced its share of laggards. Cleveland's fire warden fined James A. Stevens ten dollars for refusing to join the bucket brigade. The blaze profoundly affected the city's fire preparation and future architecture. Cleveland ordered a new fire engine and planned public reservoirs. Authorities mandated that only brick and stone could be used for new construction, a policy leading to the creation of unique buildings still standing in Cleveland's distinctive Warehouse District.

The public initially held volunteer firemen in high esteem. But a backlash developed because of firefighters' rowdy, dysfunctional and violent behavior. The young, single, working-class members of the volunteer department spent most of their days and nights at the firehouse. Neighbors complained of drinking, fighting and loud noise continuing throughout the night and into the morning. Although the volunteers worked without pay, many citizens donated money to their favorite companies, and the community paid taxes to purchase firefighting equipment and build firehouses. This financial support made the firefighters' behavior even less tolerable.

By the 1840s, citizens were often jeering and even attacking volunteer firefighters performing their duties. Throwing rocks at firemen turned into a relatively common pastime. Newspapers described interactions between firefighters and the general public as open warfare. In 1844, Cleveland's city council passed an ordinance demanding that fire marshals and constables attend every fire in order to preserve the peace. The law further stipulated that citizens must obey the orders of firemen and assist in firefighting; the penalty for noncompliance included a five-dollar fine and imprisonment. But these laws did not repress the public's fascination with harassing firemen. In 1856, the city council offered a standing fifty-dollar reward for information leading to the conviction of any person who slashed fire hoses being used to extinguish a fire.

Since each volunteer fire company responded to every alarm, intense rivalries and jealousies erupted among companies. The first group to arrive at the scene assumed the sought-after command for fighting the fire. Racing to a fire only to be relegated to supporting roles, such as relaying water to the main pumper, did not fit the mode of operation among volunteer groups. Rival companies jammed the carriage spokes of competing fire engines and even damaged or stole equipment from firehouses. When the fire alarm sounded, companies sometimes sent young boys ahead of the engines to take possession of a fire hydrant should another company arrive first. These actions often resulted in violent fights requiring resolution before work could begin on extinguishing the fire.

Competition even within the same company often erupted. Two firemen, after an 1843 parade, raced their respective engines toward the canal. The contest left one fireman with a smashed foot and the other with a broken leg. As this type of activity persisted, the press became increasingly more willing to publicize the firefighters' roles as instigators or enthusiastic participants in disorders.

Triggering false alarms, another hindrance to firefighters, reached a bizarre state in 1843 with the arrest of five Cleveland firemen charged with setting a false alarm. Four firefighters received five-dollar fines. The firemen vigorously protested the decision, claiming exemption from punishment, regardless of the crime and irrespective of their guilt or innocence. The *Cleveland Leader*, disregarding the concept of cruel and unusual punishment, offered this suggestion for dealing with people who set false alarms: "Appoint a vigilance committee whose duty it shall be to discover who the author of a false alarm is, and compel him to dress in his best clothes, if he has got any, and run all night in the middle of the muddiest street that can be found in the city of Cleveland."

The rowdy nature of the fire departments caused Cleveland to implement two controversial reforms in 1855: no unnecessary ringing of bells (polite wording that made false alarms against the law) and no card playing or other disturbances in the engine house.

Continued rivalry among companies inspired formal tournaments throughout the state and nation. In August 1858, Cleveland firefighters traveled to Fremont, capturing two prizes in a tournament including fifteen Ohio fire companies. Less than one month later, Cleveland hosted the biggest state tournament of the year; thirty-eight visiting fire companies arrived from all over the state. Marching bands, friends, relatives and members of the general public traveled to Cleveland for the contests. Cleveland companies won two of the five major competitions.

Post-tournament celebrations, continuing into the night around Public Square, turned to tragedy. Cleveland's Red Jacket Company, still in

By the turn of the twentieth century, Cleveland's fire department had developed into an organization professional in its appearance, attitude and performance. *Courtesy of Cleveland Public Library, Photograph Collection.*

uniform, attacked five members of the Deluge Company of Dayton as the visitors walked down Ontario Street past the Red Jacket firehouse. The unprovoked attack apparently resulted from the intoxicated state of the Cleveland company. One Dayton firefighter, severely cut with bottles, remained in critical condition for several days after the assault. The Red Jacket Company's rowdy behavior that evening matched its reputation. In speeding to fires, the Red Jackets had, in the past, pushed, shoved or kicked pedestrians to sidewalks or gutters. In one notorious instance, the group ran over a woman.

Nine Red Jackets faced attempted murder charges, but key witnesses failed to show up for the trial. Lacking positive identification, the court discharged all of the defendants. Many volunteer companies refused to fight fires if the Red Jacket Company continued in operation; the Cleveland City Council consequently disbanded the group. In protest, members of the dissolved company paraded through the streets of Cleveland, hanging the Cleveland fire chief in effigy as they passed his residence. In 1862, Cleveland initiated a transition from volunteers to paid firefighters. Within two years, the colorful era of volunteer groups had passed into history.

BEYOND SMOKE AND FLAMES

Seventy-six firefighters have died performing work-related duties since the Cleveland Fire Department's inception as a professional organization in 1863. Nearly one-third of these tragedies did not occur at the scene of a fire. Although training exercises and firehouse accidents claimed firefighters' lives, the most frequent cause of non-firefighting death is the dangerous task of traveling to a fire.

In the nineteenth century, the Cleveland Fire Department conducted public relations demonstrations so citizens could witness and admire the efficiency and skill of firefighters. In 1870, one such presentation required firefighters from four different locations to descend on Public Square, simulating a response to a multi-alarm fire. John C. Sturges reached his assigned position about the time a hose cart arrived directly behind him. The cart toppled unexpectedly, crushing Sturges's skull.

Just before the turn of the twentieth century, new buildings began to soar higher than firefighters' ability to protect them. Unable to reach elevated floors of increasingly taller structures, firemen watched in horror as flames consumed helpless victims. The invention of the pompier ladder narrowed the gap between building heights and firefighting capabilities. Shaped somewhat like a question mark, the ladder contained a hook on the top. Firefighters scaled the outside of a building from each successive floor by hurling the hook through a window on the next floor and pulling it into the windowsill, repeating the procedure until reaching their destination. Rescuers then placed a rope around the waists of persons trapped on upper floors, lowering them to safety. In 1888, Timothy Graham, a cadet practicing a pompier ladder drill, attempted to throw the ladder to a higher floor, but lost his balance and plunged to his death. Three years later, firefighters were lowering J.M. Ressler from the fifth floor of a training facility. The exercise simulated the rescue of people from a burning building. As Ressler reached the third floor, the rope broke. His skull was crushed from a fall of about twenty-five feet.

A trapdoor, commonly used as a quick exit from the second floor of firehouses, resulted in the 1903 death of Joseph L. Flaherty; the fireman fell through the trapdoor opening. In 1921, Patrick Jordan died after plummeting through a floor opening used for a sliding pole. In 1906, William D. Rowe returned from a fire at the downtown Cleveland Homeopathic Medical College. A streetcar struck him as he exited the fire engine in front of his station. His injuries required the amputation of his left leg, while his right leg suffered two fractures. Rowe died the day of the accident.

In the early days of Cleveland's professional fire department, the perilous task of traveling to fires claimed the lives of many firefighters. *Courtesy of Cleveland Public Library, Photograph Collection.*

Firefighters speed down Ontario Street to the scene of a fire near Public Square. A public relations simulation, similar to this actual event, resulted in the death of John C. Sturges. *Courtesy of Cleveland Public Library, Photograph Collection.*

Since 1873, seventeen firefighters have perished while traveling from their fire stations to the site of a blaze. The first such tragedy took place when Harry O. Loomis's fire wagon tipped making a sharp turn from St. Clair Avenue onto East Third Street. The firefighter jumped from the out-of-control cart, fracturing his leg in two places as he landed against a curbstone. The accident forced doctors to amputate Loomis's leg; he died from resulting complications.

In 1879, Samuel Fitch raced his hook-and-ladder truck across the old Superior Viaduct on his way to a fire in the Warehouse District. Another fire truck and a hose cart had preceded him across the overpass. Deferring to the initial truck, two ladies driving a buggy pulled off the bridge. As the buggy reentered the viaduct, it narrowly missed crashing into the hose cart. Fitch avoided an almost certain collision by swerving onto the wrong side of the road, but he crashed into an oncoming streetcar. He sustained a fatal internal injury after being hurled to the pavement. In 1887, Henry Gensert died a day after being thrown from a fire engine responding to a false alarm. Four years later, after falling from a hook-and-ladder truck, Samuel Pease fought for his life several months before his death.

The 1894 death of Willis Hizer followed an incredibly heart-wrenching ordeal. The wheel of his fire truck locked into a streetcar track as the vehicle turned onto St. Clair Avenue. Hizer fell as the fire truck lurched forward. One of the truck's wheels passed over his chest, badly crushing his body; broken bones, pressing against his heart, penetrated a lung. Engaged to be married the following week, Hizer lay dying in the hospital. His fiancée agreed to marry him immediately and care for his ten-year-old son. Opposed to the marriage, Hizer's mother created a disturbance resulting in her removal from the hospital room. A priest would not perform the ceremony because no marriage license had been obtained. After the fiancée procured the necessary paperwork, Hizer's mother attempted to sabotage the marriage by stealing the marriage license. Meanwhile, as the firefighter's condition continued to deteriorate, the attending physicians could not confirm that Hizer possessed the competence to engage in a rational act. Once again, a priest refused to perform the ceremony. Hizer died as a single man.

In 1896, Michael Walsh fell from a hose cart and died from the severe injuries he suffered. Two years later, Sylvester Esterle's fire engine raced down the steep Jefferson Street hill leading to the Flats. The fire engine struck a crosswalk barrier, hurling Esterle into the road. The engine's heavy wheels crushed his right forearm, while his right leg suffered a double fracture, tearing his leg muscles from his flesh. An ambulance transported

Herman David met his death when the firefighter's horses dragged him down the steep Dille Avenue hill. *Courtesy of the author.*

the critically injured firefighter on a bizarre odyssey encompassing three different hospitals. First, a private hospital on West Fourteenth Street refused his admission because it treated only female patients. An attendant at City Hospital, the second stop, rejected Esterle's admittance because the required paperwork did not exist. Finally, the downtown Huron Street Hospital admitted the suffering firefighter and amputated his arm. Three weeks after the accident, Esterle died of blood poisoning resulting from the operation.

In 1911, as Herman David drove his fire engine down the steep Dille Avenue hill connecting Broadway Avenue with the Flats, the engine hit a deep rut. The impact hurled David into the street while his wrists remained tightly wrapped in the loops of the reins. Unable to break free, his vehicle dragged David two hundred feet down the hill. An iron-shod hoof of one of the horses struck him in the eye, knocking him unconscious. When the reins finally broke, David landed between the front and rear wheels of the moving fire truck. One of the rear wheels ran over his stomach, crushing him to death.

James R. Killoran became the first firefighter fatality of the motorized age as gasoline-powered fire vehicles began replacing horse-drawn carts. In 1915, a new five-ton truck raced east on Central Avenue. The driver swerved to avoid hitting a wagon entering the intersection at East Forty-third Street, but the fire truck crashed into a streetcar. The impact hurled Killoran from his seat, fracturing his skull against the truck. The fire, occurring in a shed on East Sixty-first Street, proved to be minor and easily put out by hand. Two years later, William P. Rush Sr. responded to an alarm from a telegraph shanty at West Third Street. The driver of the old horse-drawn fire engine swerved to avoid being caught between two automobiles. A streetcar struck the fire engine, killing Rush.

In 1921, William J. Haley died after falling from a hook-and-ladder truck as it rounded a corner. On the day after Christmas in 1928, Arthur Stanbury and his crew raced to the scene of an explosion. Traveling west on Cedar Avenue, the fire truck careened out of control as it attempted to turn south on East Seventy-ninth Street. The rear end of the vehicle slammed into a utility pole. Stanbury leaped to avoid the accident, but as the truck tipped on its side, it pushed the fireman against the utility pole, crushing his chest and severing one of his legs.

Michael Bolivar hurried to a 1932 blaze in a home on East Seventy-seventh Street. Traveling east on St. Clair Avenue, the fire truck crashed a red light at the East Sixty-second Street intersection. A collision with a crossing hearse hurled Bolivar out of the truck and into a stopped streetcar. A defective chimney, the cause of the fire, resulted in a total monetary loss of ten dollars.

Leo A. Murphy died in a 1935 collision between a fire engine and an automobile at the intersection of Woodland Avenue and East Seventy-ninth Street. The fire engine, attempting to avoid the crash, swerved on two wheels. Murphy's flying body, thrown from the fire truck with extreme force, injured two pedestrians. The driver of the automobile, a junk peddler, said that he did not hear the warning siren. The tragedy resulted from a false alarm set by an eleven-year-old boy.

In 1945, James J. Cull died from severe head injuries and burns over his entire body, even though he never arrived at the fire. His fire truck, racing to a home on Eddy Road, crashed at a red light at the intersection of Phillips Avenue and East 123rd Street. The fire truck collided with an automobile, sideswiped a utility pole, overturned and burst into flames. As Cull landed on the sidewalk, the fire engine's gasoline tank exploded, saturating the fireman's clothing with gas. As flames ignited his garments, Cull turned into a human torch.

In 1967, as David W. Hunger's fire truck raced east on Central Avenue, the vehicle hit the rear of an automobile entering the East Fortieth Street intersection. The fire truck landed on its side, pinning Hunger between the truck and street. The call for help, originating from a firebox at East Sixty-first Street and Central Avenue, proved to be a false alarm. Five years later, Joseph A. DeCrane died when his head struck a utility pole after falling from a hook-and-ladder truck.

COLLAPSING CATASTROPHES

The focus of firefighting changed after the Civil War. Rather than primarily pouring water on fires, fire departments emphasized saving lives by aggressively entering burning buildings. The risks from structural collapse intensified with the first wave of "skyscraper" construction; fires burned hotter and longer in higher buildings.

In 1868, Paul Aukens resigned from the Cleveland Fire Department. Five years on the job had convinced him that the dangers of firefighting conflicted with caring for his wife and small child. In his new life as a painter, Aukens enjoyed evenings with his family without dreaded interruptions from fire alarms. But he still lent a helping hand to his former comrades when a special need arose; this spirit of cooperation led to Aukens's death less than a year after leaving the fire department.

Firemen called Broadway Avenue's New England Block a "huge tinderbox" even before the fatal 1869 blaze. Constructed on a steep hill, firefighters had no access to the rear of the building. Several ill-advised building additions further hampered tenants' safety. To make matters worse, the *Plain Dealer* reported that the building's upper floors housed many female residents of the "social evil circle." Insurance companies refused fire protection to a building notorious for shoddy construction and loose moral standards.

In his street-level newsstand and convenience store, C.H. Stone sold petroleum from a barrel. When he overfilled a can of oil, a few drops accidentally fell on the flame of a lamp. Recognizing the imminent danger, Stone attempted to roll the barrel away from the expanding fire. Not able to maneuver the container through a door to the street, he abandoned the burning building. The entire New England Block erupted in flames as fire ignited the lethal barrel.

Uninsured merchants and terrified residents quickly carried their most valuable belongings into the street. A heap of hats lay in the snow in front of a hat shop; mounds of commercial wallpaper and curtains sat next to residents' bedding and chairs. Before the evening ended, most of the merchandise lay in ruins, either scorched by flames or drenched by water from fire hoses. As evening arrived, cold water freezing on their clothing encased firemen in ice. A thirty-five-foot section of the building collapsed when water from fire hoses damaged supporting posts. As the building crumbled, a cooking stove and heavy timber crushed fireman Aukens.

In 1891, John Grady and Michael Howley died after sustaining injuries fighting a fire at the corner of Frankfort and Superior Avenues. The blaze began in the Standard Bottling works, one of two liquor bottling plants, along with a liquor store and salon, occupying the basement and first floor of the Short & Forman Printing Company Building. Combined with an abundant supply of alcohol, the printing company's paper, ink, oil and grease fueled the inferno as the fire spread to ten other buildings. At its peak, flames from the spectacular fire could be seen in the University Circle neighborhood. The blaze attracted more than fifteen thousand spectators, who blocked Superior Avenue and West Sixth and West Ninth Streets.

After entering from the saloon, firefighters planned to run their fire hose into the building. Grady used an axe to cut a wooden partition that impeded the route of the hose. The second floor of the building collapsed on Grady. Flames, heat, smoke and piles of brick, mortar, timber and pipes separated Grady from rescuers. Meanwhile, a firefighters' stream of water struck Howley as he stood on a ladder fighting flames. The impact hurled him through a skylight and into the private office of the printing company's president. Along with a severely burned head and face, Howley suffered internal injuries from the eighteen-foot fall. He remained conscious and in great pain during most of an unsuccessful three-week battle to remain alive.

As he attempted to exit a building, William Roth perished when the floor, roof and walls simultaneously collapsed. *Courtesy of the* Plain Dealer.

In 1899, William Roth's young son delivered breakfast to his father at the firehouse. The two would never see each other alive again. Roth responded to a fire at the Dangler Stove Corporation on Perkins Avenue. The company manufactured gas and vapor stoves, ovens and brass castings. The fire most likely started from an explosion in an elevator shaft. Momentum increased as the blaze spread to the crating department, a storage area for a large number of boxes. The fire destroyed the entire building and badly damaged the adjoining Cleveland Machine Screw Company.

Firefighters had nearly extinguished the blaze at the Cleveland Machine Screw Company when the fatal accident occurred. Roth understood his imminent danger as the building threatened to collapse. The floor, roof and walls gave way just before Roth, the last fireman attempting to leave, could depart. Roth's groans could be heard as rescuers removed tons of debris that had crushed the fireman. Heavy timber even prevented firemen from removing his body.

Although Patrick H. Joyce's reputation for bravery rivaled that of his older brother, a captain in the Cleveland Fire Department, a collapsing wall cut short the younger Joyce's career and life. In 1902, fire broke out in a building on the corner of East Fortieth Street and Hamilton Avenue. After bringing the major blaze under control, five firemen battled a small remaining fire. Without warning, one of the building's walls collapsed, burying all five firefighters. Against amazing odds, four survived. About five thousand people gathered to watch the blaze and interfered with the firefighters' work. Police used clubs to prevent the onlookers from forcing their way into the ruins to help search for Joyce. Captain William J. Joyce joined other members of the fire department in search of his brother. After several hours, rescuers finally found his lifeless body crushed by a piece of machinery.

In 1903, fire destroyed the Cleveland Electric Company's two-acre streetcar barns located at Holmden Avenue and West Twenty-fifth Street. A spark in the wires of one of the seventy-three streetcars located in the barns probably started the blaze. James Schweda, Robert Duffy and Robert Reid died in an avalanche of hot bricks, created by a falling wall. Schweda died instantly when the ruins crushed his head. Duffy, still alive when rescuers found him, requested a priest. He smiled as a clergyman from St. Wenceslas Church arrived; he died in the arms of the priest from a broken back, a broken leg and a crushed chest. Suffering from a crushed head and broken ribs, Reid asked, "Are the other boys out?" when the rescuers reached him. Those proved to be his last words.

Fred Brown fought a 1935 blaze at the Atlas Steel & Supply Company on Trumbull Avenue. Several tons of brick and steel from a collapsing wall buried Brown, who died from a fractured skull and crushed chest. In 1944, rubble from an exploding fourteen-foot tile wall in Cleveland's west side stockyards killed Patrick J. Mangan and Norman H. Kitzerow. As flames consumed a meat-processing building, the explosion occurred when another set of firefighters blasted the burning building with a stream of water.

In 1947, Theodore Brenyas died attempting to save the burning Franklin Boulevard Methodist Church as one-hundred-foot flames, visible from Public Square, spread to the steeple. The wooden framework of the eighty-year-old church gave way, weakening the rear wall in the process. Five tons of brick buried Brenyas as the wall collapsed. The following year, a falling brick wall killed Paul I. Green and Henry Spencer. That fire, of unknown origin, struck the Russo Wine Company on Lorain Avenue. Alcohol fumes from forty thousand cases of wine, along with paper cartons and labels, intensified the blaze.

Robert J. Termansky died in 1963 under an avalanche of concrete in a three-story apartment on East Eighty-fifth Street. Tenants escaped using a ladder set up in a narrow space between the apartment and a nearly adjoining building. When the top of the ladder caught fire, Termansky struggled to move it even as a portion of the building collapsed on him.

While Edward J. Gresky Jr. and his wife enjoyed dinner, he told her, "You have so little time, you should spend it doing the nicest and kindest things you can do for people." Three days later, he died fighting a 1974 fire in a vacant building on West Ninth Street. Intense flames prevented frustrated firemen from reaching Gresky, who had fallen through the first floor into the building's basement.

COURAGEOUS HEARTS

Born in England, William A. Reynolds moved to Cleveland as a child. After fighting in the Civil War, he joined the Cleveland Fire Department in 1871 but resigned in 1882 to pursue business interests in Canada. Four years later, Reynolds returned to the fire department. In 1897, while traveling to a residential fire on Starkweather Avenue, he experienced difficulty as he reached for his fire helmet and coat. Arriving at the fire scene, Reynolds jumped from a still-moving fire truck, leaped over a fence, entered the

Sheldon Writhe died of a heart attack following his successful battle with a fire in a storage company. *Courtesy of the* Plain Dealer.

burning home and died as he exited the house, the first of fifteen Cleveland firemen to suffer fatal heart attacks caused by their strenuous jobs.

In 1901, lightning created a fire at a storage company on Scranton Road. Sheldon Wright's position on the roof of the five-story building subjected him to the extremely dense smoke pouring from the windows and skylight. After leaving the fire, Wright traveled to the fire department headquarters in city hall. From there he went to his fire station on St. Clair Avenue. Although Wright complained of chest pains, he prepared a bath at the fire station. Wright died of heart failure in the bathroom.

Daniel O'Loughlin fought a 1932 fire in the Century Power Building on Frankfort Avenue. Beginning on the fourth floor, the blaze spread down an elevator shaft and stairwell. Falling timber smashed two water mains inside the building. Along with the loss of the large amount of water needed to fight the fire, the broken mains contributed to flooding the nearby sewers. Witnesses described Frankfort Avenue as a canal with firemen wading in knee-deep water. O'Loughlin, wet and cold, complained of chills that turned into pneumonia. Members of the fire department visited his home and provided oxygen to alleviate the pneumonia. Although his condition improved, O'Loughlin's heart failed. He died four days after the fire.

A dilapidated skating rink remained as the only remnant of Luna Park, a former amusement park at Woodland Avenue and East Ninety-third Street. In 1938, neighbors attempted for the seventh time to burn down the eyesore by igniting oil-soaked rags and paper stuffed under the walls and floor of the building. Waiting more than an hour to report the fire, residents shouted, "Let it burn!" to the firefighters. The blaze turned out to be more serious than the amateur arsonists had planned. Intense heat melted telephone and electric lines, while wind carried the fire into the street, threatening nearby homes. The efforts of Roy Haylor and his comrades may have saved the entire neighborhood from destruction. After the fire, Haylor stopped for a cup of coffee and died of a heart attack as he began the trip back to the fire station.

A 1949 fire in a Euclid Avenue manufacturing facility making children's furniture began among piles of upholstering material. John J. Kilbane died from heart failure as he connected a hose to a fire hydrant. Henry F. Lange also died from heart failure that year. A violinist, Lange once conducted a local orchestra that performed on cruise ships. In addition, he operated a cigar shop on West Twenty-fifth Street before beginning his firefighting career. His death arose as he directed cleanup operations after a garage fire on St. Clair Avenue. The year before, the sixty-four-year-old had missed his first day of work.

In 1956, an electrical wire, downed by a strong wind, landed on the fire escape of the Saron Packaging Company Plant on West Thirty-third Street. A spark from the wire developed into an undetected smoldering fire. In less than an hour, the ensuing blaze threatened the business and the nearby residential neighborhood. Sixty-three-year-old Joseph Vlasty handled pumps for eight hours before dying of a heart attack while cleaning debris after the fire. Three years later, Jack W. Poe suffered a fatal heart attack inside the burning Ideal Macaroni Company Building at East Twenty-second Street and Scoville Avenue. At the time of the fire, the structure stood ready to be demolished for the Inner Belt freeway construction.

A 1960 fire began in the basement of the four-story apartment on East Ninetieth Street, just north of Chester Avenue. The blaze raced through the building's clothes chutes, spreading almost simultaneously to every floor. Charles A. Prymmer died of a heart attack while carrying a generator into the burning apartment building. Three years later, John J. Finucan fought a fire in a three-family dwelling on Somerset Avenue. A biting cold had frozen the two closest fire hydrants. Finucan raced down the street to plug his hose into the nearest usable hydrant. He then ran inside the building to help fight the fire. The exertion, combined with the sudden temperature change, precipitated his fatal heart attack.

Kenneth F. Jacklitz studied law and passed the bar exam while employed as a fireman. Before he had the opportunity to launch his law career, he fought a 1963 fire in the vacant Penn Square Hotel on East Fifty-fifth Street. Vagrants occupying the building started the blaze in an attempt to keep warm. Jacklitz hauled a hose up a ladder to the third floor. His heart failed from the physical activity combined with a severe temperature change.

In 1969, George J. Solloway died of a heart attack while fighting a fire at the Smerda Music House on Broadway Avenue. Also that year, a wooden beam, too close to a chimney, caused a fire at the St. Anthony Home for Boys on Detroit Avenue. John J. Gallagher, a forty-three-year veteran of the fire department, collapsed at the scene, suffering a heart attack. A fireman revived him, but he died of a second attack at the hospital.

In 1970, thirty-six-year-old Salvatore Mazzola, the youngest firefighter to die from heart failure on the job, fought a fire in a vacant home on East 147th Street. After returning to the fire station, he collapsed and died. Frank L. Bonacci's heart failed as he attached a hose to a hydrant while battling a 1972 fire in an apartment building.

Smoke, Fumes and Explosions

Far more firefighters die from smoke inhalation than from burns. In 1879, John F. Maher died of consumption contracted from weakened lungs, the result of exposure to smoke inhalation from a fire. John T. Gillson, a former carriage painter and member of a volunteer fire department, joined the paid department after fighting in the Civil War. In 1882, he died of heart, lung and kidney problems after inhaling nitric acid fumes fighting a fire at an industrial plant. Sadly, his fire extinguisher had generated the lethal fumes.

In 1897, a can of benzene, used to clean printing equipment, exploded in the pressroom of a printing and lithographing establishment on Frankfort Avenue. Battling strong northwest winds and bitter cold, firefighters waged a five-hour fight to control the blaze. Water directed at the inferno frequently turned to icicles before arriving at its intended destination and then changed into steam because of the fire's intense heat. Disoriented by blinding smoke, William B. MacFeeters plunged thirty feet through an elevator shaft to his death.

While fighting a 1923 fire, Walter J. Read died of carbon monoxide poisoning created from smoke inhalation. The death of thirty-two-year veteran Charles W. Klocksen in 1943 took place as he saved a fellow firefighter from certain doom. Grease-coated work clothes, stuffed in lockers, fueled a fire at the Oster Manufacturing plant. Through dense smoke, Klocksen guided a fireman out of the building but died from breathing the smoke. In 1962, Walter A. Kress collapsed as he fought a grass fire on West Forty-eighth Street.

Three nights each week, Stanley Lawson attended classes to prepare himself for a job as a draftsman following his planned retirement from the fire department. In 1966, he scheduled both Christmas Eve and Christmas Day as vacation time. His wife, a restaurant hostess, arranged Christmas Day off, marking the first time the couple and their three sons would spend the holiday together. However, on Christmas Eve, a tenant fell asleep while smoking in a West Twenty-fifth Street apartment and forced Lawson back to work. The firefighters extinguished the blaze by throwing a mattress and box springs from a window. But Lawson incorrectly believed that someone remained trapped in an upper-floor bedroom. He died of smoke inhalation during an ill-fated rescue attempt.

After collapsing at a 1969 fire in a commercial garage, John D. Ruszkowski never regained consciousness and died two weeks later. John W. McNamee

William B. MacFeeters died at a fire site by falling through an elevator shaft. *Courtesy of the* Plain Dealer.

died in 1974 at the scene of a fire at the Hawley House, a downtown hotel. After two heroic rescue operations, he perished from smoke inhalation while attempting a third mission. In 1985, Daniel R. Pescatrice entered the burning Milner Electric Company on St. Clair Avenue. Dense smoke disoriented him as he moved among tight rows of floor-to-ceiling storage racks. He radioed for help when his oxygen tank emptied, but rescuers could not locate him in the maze of racks.

Eleven other firemen died at the scene of a fire as a result of circumstances other than burns. The first, Henry C. Harmon Jr., had followed admirably in his father's footsteps. Beginning as a substitute fireman in 1874, he spent five years working his way into a permanent position. Harmon's father served in the same company when the son raced to an 1884 fire on Public Square—a gas explosion had turned the newly constructed Wick Building into an inferno. The blaze spread to the Old Stone Church located next door. Harmon, attempting to stop the fire in the burning church, fought the blaze from the church's steeple. Water from the fire engines blasted high into the air, much of it landing on the firefighters. Their protective clothing, covered with ice, became frozen stiff. After the fire, Harmon complained of pain in his limbs. He remained on duty, but his health grew progressively worse. Four days after the fire, his comrades carried Harmon in a blanket to his home, where he died five days later. The fatality resulted from rheumatic fever induced by exposure to the cold weather and water.

Edwin J. Hart, pictured with his family, died in 1963 when a truck exploded during a garage fire. *Courtesy of Cleveland Public Library, Photograph Collection.*

John T. McKenna perished when hit by debris in the explosion that also killed Edwin J. Hart. *Courtesy of Cleveland Public Library, Photograph Collection.*

Two explosions, within three years of each other, claimed the lives of eight firemen—each incident killed four firefighters. In 1963, a customer using a truck to deliver propane brought the vehicle to a downtown garage for repairs. Somewhere between 50 and 100 gallons of propane remained in the truck's 1,500-gallon tank. Working at the garage, an off-duty fireman spotted a leak in a valve near the rear of the truck. Employees evacuated the building and summoned the fire department. Two fire stations, each located within one mile of the garage, responded too quickly. The building exploded almost immediately after their arrival. If the firemen had arrived only two minutes later, none would have died.

The explosion demolished the garage, sent the roof falling as the walls collapsed and blew the hood off a fire truck. Two firemen died on the scene. Edwin J. Hart, standing next to the deadly truck when the explosion occurred, had no chance for survival. Falling debris killed John T. McKenna. Two days later, Robert H. Jones died from head injuries sustained when a flying brick struck him. He never regained consciousness after the accident. Robert L. Marquard suffered first- and second-degree burns over 60 percent of his body and died two weeks later.

Metallurgical Inc. processed manganese and aluminum used in the production of steel. The manufacturing operation created a highly explosive aluminum dust. In 1966, as workers installed a new dust collector, welders cut ductwork to allow the dismantling of an older dust-collecting device. A spark from a welding torch set off a fire that employees battled for about thirty minutes before calling the fire department.

Although firefighters appeared to have extinguished the blaze, four remained inside the plant for another forty-five minutes. Then, an unexpected explosion tore holes in the roof of the fifty-foot-high building. All four died from the resulting intense heat. In addition to creating four widows, the blaze also left twelve young children and two grown offspring without fathers. Joseph G. Toolis left five children, four sons and one daughter, ranging in age from

During a 1968 residential fire, Dennis J. Connors suffered fatal head injuries by falling through a floor. *Courtesy of Cleveland Public Library, Photograph Collection.*

six days to eight years. John A. Petz had three boys and two girls. Charles G. Doehner had two sons. Ralph E. Simon, who had survived the garage explosion three years earlier, had an adult son and daughter.

Two other firefighters' deaths resulted from accidents at fire scenes. In 1968, Dennis J. Connors died of head injuries after falling through a floor in a home on Erwin Avenue where children playing with matches had created a blaze. In 1977, Edward M. Carey fell on a rotting step during a fire at Barkwell School. As a result of oxygen deprivation, Carey remained in a coma for more than fifteen years prior to his 1995 death.

Part VI

DANGER FROM ABOVE

WICKED WINDS

Violent winds have generated Cleveland storms worthy of the nicknames "devil wind" and "baby cyclone." From severe localized gusts to the widespread Superstorm Sandy, wind has been a frequent and sometimes unexpectedly deadly force contributing to the city's weather calamities.

As Leonard Endress walked from his downtown workplace to purchase a steak for lunch, a violent 1868 wind sent an advertising sign flying through Public Square and into his head. He died instantly from a crushed skull. In an 1893 windstorm, three deaths occurred when a scaffold collapsed at the rolling mills in Cleveland's southeast side. The storm destroyed a home at the corner of East 107th Street and Superior Avenue when falling debris killed another person.

A seemingly mild spring thunderstorm, passing through Cleveland in 1909, suddenly developed into a sixty-six-mile-per-hour gale ripping a two-mile-wide and six-mile-long path through Cleveland. Although the storm's peak lasted only five minutes, the wind caused the deaths of six people. The youngest, seven-year-old Arthur Niedbalski, died after being hit by bricks from a falling steeple at St. Stanislas Church. In the B&O train yards, wind blew Clarence Troutman from a boxcar, whereupon a switch engine ran over him. Joseph Convell perished falling from a crane at the Cleveland Furnace Company. Blowing material at the Cleveland Crossing Company crushed Joseph E. Vessla. A stone from the roof of the State Hospital for the Insane

A violent 1909 windstorm destroyed two 232-foot steeples at St. Stanislaus Church. A young boy, walking on the sidewalk, died when bricks from one of the falling steeples struck him. *Author's collection.*

struck and killed Olive Phalen, a hospital nurse. Working as a caddy at the Euclid Club, Louis Petro died when a building collapsed. Frightened by the wind, Fred Grugel committed suicide by drinking carbolic acid. Lacking the characteristic funnel shape of a true tornado, a meteorologist described the tempest as "a thunderstorm of exceptional violence."

In 1951, a ninety-mile-per-hour wind, described as a "baby cyclone," blasted a ten-block area near the intersection of West 130th Street and Bellaire Road. The fierce wind drove fragments of wood into a brick wall and propelled a garage 150 feet through the air. One resident retrieved the family car exactly where it had been parked, but the accompanying garage had vanished during the storm. The four-minute storm's narrow path, twenty yards in width and one hundred yards in length, created no injuries. In a very peculiar incident, the windstorm transported a school of fish onto the roof of a garage. Strong updrafts within windstorms sometimes grab hold of fish, frogs, and birds, all of which return to earth as the updraft subsides. Under very extreme circumstances, raining cats and dogs may actually be possible.

In 1956, Daniel and Ethel Adams, along with their two young boys (seven-year-old Robert and four-year-old Leonard) dined at the Scenery Tavern on Pearl Road. Joseph and Velma Peets, celebrating their wedding anniversary,

A home once standing at 3241 Meyer Avenue is in ruins after a 1956 windstorm. The street is south of Clark Avenue between Scranton and Fulton Roads. *Courtesy of Cleveland Public Library, Photograph Collection.*

joined the Adams family. An evening cloudburst produced a one-hundred-mile-per-hour wind gust that collapsed the walls and ceiling of the tavern, crushing to death both boys and twenty-eight-year-old Joseph Peets. On another part of the west side, nineteen-year-old Sidney Odom, driving home with an ice cream treat for the family, died as a falling tree demolished his car on Lake Road. George Balogh returned home safely from working a late shift at a General Motors plant, although toppled trees prevented him from driving his automobile the entire distance. When Balogh returned to inspect the condition of his car, a fallen wire electrocuted him. Frank Marohnic died after touching a wire while helping his neighbors clean up storm debris. In Lakewood, an amateur meteorologist witnessed his wind gauge register one hundred miles per hour before it blew away. Not bearing the characteristics of a tornado, the storm is known as "the devil wind" in Cleveland folklore.

A severe 1962 thunderstorm caused wind gusts peaking officially at 104 miles per hour at Burke Airport. Three workers at the Monarch Aluminum Manufacturing Company on Detroit Avenue died when a fifty-thousand-gallon water tower crashed through five floors of the building. In another tragedy, a father of six children died when he touched a live wire buried under a pile of leaves in his driveway. A forty-foot tear in the tent of Musicarnival, a popular summer theater, resulted in rain completely drenching patrons enjoying a performance of *The Desert Song*. A wedding reception in a Denison

In April 1975, pedestrians grab a utility pole to prevent being blown into the street. *Courtesy of Cleveland Public Library, Photograph Collection.*

Avenue hall continued by candlelight after the power failed. Although guests remained safe in the building, a falling tree crushed three automobiles in the parking lot.

Despite the 450-mile distance from Superstorm Sandy's landfall along the New Jersey coast, the 2012 tempest walloped Cleveland with rain and near-hurricane-strength winds. Ferociously traveling across Lake Erie, the storm created twenty-foot waves, while rain penetrated window frames in downtown buildings. The water-soaked Shoreway closed in both directions between East Fifty-fifth and East Seventy-second Streets, while malfunctioning traffic signals on St. Clair Avenue, the recommended alternate route, completely stopped rush-hour traffic. Wind and water damaged downtown office and apartment buildings, while Cleveland State University students vacated the storm-damaged Fenn Tower dorm. The hurricane's damage to Gordon Park warranted a federal government disaster relief grant. Liberating a bit of Cleveland nostalgia, Sandy returned to the shoreline a set of old bricks from Cleveland's former Municipal Stadium; the bricks currently serve as reefs buried in Lake Erie.

Visitors from the Sky

Although comets and meteors have fascinated and frightened Clevelanders since the city's founding, speculation surrounding the 1910 visit of Halley's Comet reached a near-fever pitch. Newspapers warned that the comet might set the entire world on fire; at a minimum, global poisoning could be expected. As the day of the expected arrival neared, many Clevelanders suffered increasing uneasiness. When a gust of wind blew out a window in downtown's Tellings Restaurant, a customer observed a minister seated nearby and screamed, "Save me from the comet!"

Cleveland entered an advanced state of preparation as the comet's closest encounter with Earth drew nearer. Churches added special prayer meetings, saloons increased their inventory of beer and liquor and dancehalls expanded hours of operation. Parents, fearing the end of the world, forbade their children from attending school. Among businesspeople, not everyone believed that the planet neared obliteration. The Wamelink & Sons Piano Company advertised, "Halley's Comet Is Due to Approach the Earth Today," but noted that while interest in the comet would pass, a piano offered lasting joy. Prices for Hardman pianos in mahogany cabinets,

In 1910, as Halley's Comet approached Earth, an astronomer predicted that the comet's gas "would impregnate the atmosphere and possibly snuff out all life on the planet." *Courtesy of Cleveland Public Library, Photograph Collection.*

used only for demonstration purposes, dropped from $850 to $700 during a special comet sale. Luna Amusement Park hired an illumination expert to produce a simulation of a comet rushing through space. The creation, not quite as authentic as the advertising promised, still produced large crowds who enjoyed a concurrent fireworks display.

Cleveland residents on the near west side may have been particularly apprehensive. A falling meteor, heralding the comet's arrival, struck the ground at West Seventy-third and Grace Avenue. Residents reported a hissing sound, multicolored light and an explosion as the meteor hit the street's brick pavement. Curiosity seekers found the remnants too hot to touch.

Finally, on the night of May 18, the comet reached its closest distance to Earth. Many Clevelanders approached the evening in a festive and jovial state of mind. In almost every neighborhood, thousands of residents walked down the middle of streets to obtain a better look at the comet. Fortunately, neither Cleveland nor the rest of the planet suffered any ill effects from the passing of Halley's Comet.

Meteors, commonly called falling or shooting stars, appear as fast-moving streaks, rarely visible for more than a few seconds. On the evening of July 20,

1860, the greatest meteor shower ever seen in North America passed across Lake Erie. Rising above the northwest horizon, the shower increased in size until it resembled a full moon. The pale white light caused shadows from Cleveland's downtown buildings at 9:00 p.m. On July 11, 1939, residents of Ohio, Michigan, Indiana, Pennsylvania, New York and Ontario witnessed a huge meteor. Observers thought that they had seen an airplane on fire or the aftermath of an ore boat explosion. Inspired by the event, *Cleveland Press* science editor David Dietz composed an article headlined, "Bombs from the

A 1952 U.S. Coast Guard photograph illustrates possible flying saucers hovering over Massachusetts. Similar sightings transformed northeast Ohio into a hotbed for UFO investigations. *Courtesy of Cleveland Public Library, Photograph Collection.*

Sky." He suggested that an even larger meteor could appear at any second, with the power to annihilate the entire city of Cleveland.

After comprehending the existence and characteristics of comets and meteors, scientists and laymen faced a new challenge. Over the decades, northeast Ohio has remained a hotbed for UFO sightings. Founded in 1952, the still-existing Cleveland UFOlogy Project investigates UFO activity. Beginning in members' living rooms, meeting places have included the Central YMCA, a Red Cross facility, a bank meeting room, a church basement, Tri-C, a funeral home and a yoga studio. This is the oldest such organization in the United States, most likely the world. In the 1960s, Clevelanders formed three active UFO organizations and hosted the first major national UFO convention.

Cleveland's involvement with unidentified flying object sightings began in 1952. Ralph Mayher, a cameraman for a Cleveland television station, photographed what appeared to be a flying saucer. Agents from the Central Intelligence Agency (CIA) interviewed Mayher after he had surrendered his film to Air Force Intelligence. An official finding concluded that Mayher had filmed a meteor.

In 1955, dozens of motorists on the Ohio Turnpike reported the landing of a spaceship on the new toll road. In actuality, high winds had overturned a truck containing a plastic swimming pool, which sailed through the air before staging a dramatic landing on a turnpike pole. Sightings became much more credible as the decades progressed.

One of the best-documented and most discussed encounters with an unidentified flying object began in 1966 in Portage County. Two police officers, observing a disc-shaped object, followed the UFO at speeds up to one hundred miles per hour for about thirty minutes. Patrolmen from East Palestine, Ohio and Conway, Pennsylvania, also viewed the object and joined the pursuit. Officially, the United States Air Force surmised that the police officers had chased images of an Echo communications satellite and the planet Venus, mistakenly believing both to be the same object. The air force explained the UFO's unusual maneuvers as optical illusions created by the excitement of the police and the high speed of travel.

In 1973, a four-person crew in a United States Army Reserve helicopter departed Columbus for Cleveland Hopkins Airport. About ten miles south of Mansfield, a red light startled the crew. Turning toward the helicopter, the light appeared to be on a collision course. Even when the crew placed the helicopter into a sharp descent, the red light continued to close in. Just as a crash appeared imminent, the unknown object completely stopped in midair. After a wait of about ten seconds, each crewmember observed the object making an abrupt forty-five-degree turn as it proceeded toward Lake Erie; no known aircraft could have made such a sharp turn. Several civilians reported seeing a strange red light in the sky at the same time as the helicopter's odd encounter.

In 1988, witnesses observed a large, gray, blimp-like object with bright white lights above Lake Erie near the Perry Nuclear Plant. The object discharged five or six yellow, triangular lights from its side. The triangles initially hovered around the pseudo-blimp before departing at speeds much faster than possible with any known aircraft. The triangles returned to the larger ship about an hour later. The object then landed on the Lake Erie ice. Independent witnesses provided corroborating reports of the bizarre event. An initial Coast Guard report confirmed that two personnel witnessed the lights and a large object dispersing smaller flying objects. A later report explained the sightings as confusion with the closely aligned planets Venus and Jupiter. Gases in the atmosphere accounted for the flashing lights and smaller objects.

In 1994, five police departments tracked a red, saucer-shaped object. The Liberty Township, Howland, Hubbard and Girard Police Departments, along with the Trumbull County Sheriff's Department, pursued the UFO for several hours. Families in two bordering residential neighborhoods stood in the streets viewing the object. A Trumbull County dispatcher confirmed receiving many telephone calls regarding it. An NBC television special concerning UFOs broadcast audio excerpts from Trumbull County in which the dispatcher openly discussed the sightings with multiple police officers as they witnessed the UFOs in flight.

Reports of UFOs in northeast Ohio have continued unabated into the twenty-first century, including much-publicized sightings in Olmsted Falls and Strongsville. Ted Henry, one of Cleveland's respected newscasters, is among the individuals reporting UFO sightings. Greater Cleveland added a new dimension to its UFO activities when Phyllis Budinger, a retired scientist, established a laboratory to examine physical evidence related to UFOs. She has evaluated evidence in many high-profile cases.

Part VII

CONQUERING DISEASE

A REIGN OF TERROR

In 1832, the steamship *Henry Clay* transported military troops (fighting in the Black Hawk Indian War) from Buffalo to Chicago. Stricken with an outbreak of cholera and seeking food and medicine, the ship sought refuge in Detroit, but the city blocked its entry. Returning east and flying a distress flag, the *Henry Clay* docked on the west bank of the Cuyahoga River. Crewmen found asylum in barracks, where physicians attended to them. The ship returned to Buffalo, but not before introducing Cleveland to the dreaded disease; cholera raged near the river for eight weeks. The city established a hospital on Whiskey Island to treat victims, but 64 citizens still died. Two years later, cholera claimed the lives of about 100 of Cleveland's 4,300 inhabitants. A severe 1849 attack resulted in 130 deaths.

No one understood the origin of cholera, but a local newspaper noted that the disease seemed to strike foreigners, Irishmen or people living in filthy quarters. Peddlers provided Clevelanders with dubious preventative options. Mr. Fiske and Mr. Hall promoted their ginger syrup to inhibit cholera, while J. Eldrehi advertised amulet necklaces "of fresh bloom with a very fine odor" to provide excellent protection against contagious diseases. The necklaces ranged in price from one to four dollars.

Many doctors believed that poisonous gases, originating in sewers, swamps and garbage pits, caused cholera, while decaying vegetables at the canal's bottom supposedly created local epidemics. Other explanations included deficiency of electricity in the atmosphere, residents not building homes on sand foundations, consumption of fruits and vegetables and the absence of thinking. A letter to a Cleveland newspaper provided evidence of the later cause: "Few physicians or nurses perish in cholera epidemics. The fact that their minds are employed seems to keep them immune."

Dr. Edward Seguin, a local doctor, offered this analysis of the disease: "Cholera is found in the baskets of farmers in the markets. The monster appears in the attractive form of green gooseberries, half-ripe cherries, and potatoes scarcely formed. Tomorrow, it will be gripping the bowels of many imprudent eaters. Where is the Board of Health? They should put an end to this excess of greenness." The fruit and vegetable theory remained in vogue for years, as witnessed in this remark in an 1870 *Cleveland Leader* editorial: "Until the last melon and cucumber, the last of the green apples, the sour plums and bruised pears have disappeared, there will yet be a chance for cholera." Although not recognized at the time, cholera had already lost its deadly grip on Clevelanders.

Spread by untreated diarrhea and tainted feces, cholera infected waterways and groundwater that eventually contaminated well water. Cleveland's first settlers unknowingly contracted cholera by drinking infected well water and

The Kentucky Street Reservoir behind the pumping station, part of Cleveland's first centralized water system, helped eliminate dreaded cholera attacks in Cleveland. *Courtesy of Cleveland Public Library, Photograph Collection.*

propagated the disease with poor hygienic habits. By 1840, the city's population had increased to 6,071. Cleveland's initial attempt to keep pace with a growing demand for water did nothing to prevent cholera; city officials allotted thirty-five dollars to dig a well on Public Square.

In the 1850s, the city constructed its first centralized water system. About three hundred feet from Lake Erie's shore, a fifty-inch-diameter pipe accumulated water, which a pumping station collected and sent to a 5-million-gallon reservoir located on Kentucky Street (West Thirty-eighth Street) in Ohio City. An eleven-mile infrastructure of pipes distributed the water from the reservoir to Cleveland's homes and businesses. The system delivered about thirty-eight thousand gallons of water each day and, in the process, ended cholera attacks originating in Cleveland. The new water system inadvertently eliminated the cholera threat by reducing the demand for infected well water.

While inhibiting cholera, the new water system did little to alleviate the increase of typhoid fever. Cleveland's first serious encounter with this killer disease occurred in 1827—seventeen citizens died among a population of fewer than one thousand. At the time, doctors believed that soil disturbances during the canal excavation caused typhoid fever. But attacks continued for more than a century after the canal's completion. For many stricken with the disease, the treatment proved worse than the illness. Supposed cures often involved draining the body of fluids and prescribing medicines that are now classified as poisons. Doctors routinely recommended calomel, a powder containing mercury that subjected patients to lethal mercury poisoning.

Consumption of contaminated food or water causes both cholera and typhoid fever. Elimination of widespread use of well water ended the cholera menace, while typhoid fever continued because a human carrier, rather than a well, spread the disease. Carriers discharge typhoid bacteria in their feces and urine; even today, poor hygiene creates contamination. But in the nineteenth century, Cleveland's sewer-infested water system transported the disease throughout the city.

From 1868 to 1898, Cleveland collected garbage, deposited the accumulation on a barge in the Cuyahoga River and dumped the contents into Lake Erie. Meanwhile, raw sewage flowed freely from streams into the lake. Although few disputed the lake's polluted condition, suggested remedies may appear strange to today's more environmentally conscious citizens. In 1872, the *Cleveland Leader* provided this advice: "Our drinking water is horrible. The benzene contained in it is sufficient to create disease among the citizens who are obliged to swallow it. The best course for the

Into the early twentieth century, the poor condition of Cleveland's water motivated thousands of residents to visit "natural" park springs, where they filled bottles with perceived purer water. *Author's collection.*

Opposite: In 1925, the Fairmount Pumping Station, near University Circle, began pumping filtered water into Cleveland's homes and businesses. *Courtesy of Cleveland Public Library, Photograph Collection.*

people to pursue is probably to grin and bear it." Clevelanders attempted to secure "pure" drinking water from springs in public parks, but the spring water contained its own sets of contaminates.

As far as rectifying the city's impure water system, the thought of eliminating pollutants did not seem to be a viable alternative. Instead, the solution involved continually drawing water farther from Lake Erie's shore. The *Cleveland Leader* clarified the situation: "Only one remedy exists: Water pipes supplying the reservoir must be moved to some point where this poison will not drift, either extended much further into the lake or located at least a mile farther from the river."

In 1895, Dr. Ohlmacher of the Wooster Medical School conducted a study to measure the quality of the drinking water in Cleveland. The *Plain Dealer* reported his results using the headline, "Death in Water" and the byline, "Dr. Ohlmacher Shows that Lake Water Is Poisonous." The doctor used test tubes, decanters and vials to demonstrate that every fifteen drops of Cleveland drinking water contained more than ten thousand germs, ten times the amount considered dangerous. That same year, a Cleveland doctor told the local chamber of commerce, "Researchers of today show that the

Built in 1904 and expanded in 1927, the Kirtland Pumping Station, on East Forty-ninth Street at the lakefront, completed Cleveland's dramatic expansion of water facilities during the 1920s. *Author's collection.*

Opposite, top: The Baldwin Filtration Plant's research laboratory, combined with the nearby Fairmount Reservoir, enhanced Cleveland's reputation as a provider of excellent city water. *Courtesy of Cleveland Public Library, Photograph Collection.*

Opposite, bottom: Carved out of solid rock, the Fairmount Reservoir is a staging area for water treated at the Baldwin Filtration Plant (left). *Courtesy of Cleveland Public Library, Photograph Collection.*

dreaded typhoid bacillus is nothing more or less than bacillus contained in human excrement."

Cleveland implemented major improvements in water quality in the second decade of the twentieth century. In 1911, the city added chlorine (later to be replaced by fluoride) to water; daily testing of water quality began in 1913. These improvements significantly reduced typhoid fever occurrences. Yet the advances did not prevent millions of gallons of raw sewage from being dumped into Lake Erie and the Cuyahoga River. In the 1920s, Cleveland introduced impressive improvements in water filtration, dramatically reducing cases of typhoid fever.

As late as 1931, six inmates of the Cleveland State Hospital for the Insane died in a typhoid fever attack. In 1944, another outbreak occurred due to improper handling of orange juice by a downtown hotel worker. By the 1950s, the elimination of raw sewage dumped into lakes and rivers, improved water filtration and testing, more sophisticated sewer systems and water treatment facilities, effective vaccinations and greater public awareness of sanitation issues all combined to successfully eliminate the major threat of typhoid fever.

THE WORLD'S GREATEST PANDEMIC

In 1918, even though only one case of influenza had been reported in Cleveland through mid-September, city officials understood the grave threat. Deemed a precautionary measure, City Hospital prepared extra wards for potential flu victims. Health experts told Clevelanders, "Every person must become an unofficial health officer charged with the responsibility of seeing to it that the disease will not gain ground in Cleveland." Cleveland's police chief issued the following statement to his organization: "Every member of the police department must understand that it is just as important to arrest people who spit on streets, sidewalks, and streetcars as it is to apprehend burglars and thieves. Violators must be immediately arrested and brought into court for prosecution."

Despite the warnings, by mid-October, Cleveland had registered more than five thousand cases of influenza, fifty of these resulting in death. Nothing impeded the relentless advancement of the dreaded epidemic that

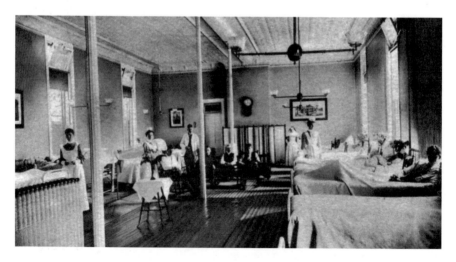

During the 1918 influenza epidemic, medical staffs worked long hours in crowded conditions. In this scene, nurses attend to patients at St. Vincent Hospital. *Author's collection.*

eventually took the lives of 3,474 Clevelanders. Throughout the world, the scourge created the most severe outbreak of disease in human history, killing somewhere between 50 and 100 million people.

On October 14, Warner School reported that 323 of its 800 students failed to attend classes. As the influenza spread, all Cleveland public schools closed the next day. The city threatened to arrest any undertaker holding a public funeral; only family and immediate relatives received permission to attend interments. A homeowner creating a cloud of dust while sweeping a sidewalk faced arrest; health officials reasoned that "the dust swept from sidewalks floats through the air for hours and carries within it hundreds of influenza germs." Police arrested the mayor of Akron for participating in a public meeting to celebrate the opening of a new streetcar line.

Churches, libraries, theaters, dance halls, billiard rooms, pool halls, bowling alleys and cabarets shut down; other bans forbade all public meetings, including weddings. The clergy supported the closing of churches but questioned why bars remained open. Stranded actors obtained temporary work in ammunition plants. The Priscilla Theater, located on East Ninth Street, served meals to all

Volunteers at a street kitchen served food to children of families afflicted by the 1918 influenza outbreak. *Courtesy of Cleveland Public Library, Photograph Collection.*

out-of-work actresses. Female performers obtained food and shelter in private homes; men seemed especially charitable toward the fifty-four chorus girls appearing in five musical tabloids when the theaters closed.

By October 24, the regular crew of twenty-six gravediggers at Calvary Cemetery could not keep pace with the demand for new burial places. Relatives and friends of the dead helped dig the graves, while steam shovels created larger burial places accommodating multiple caskets. The difficulty of obtaining jurors caused postponement of civil court cases. Cleveland courts closed, except for probate, juvenile and municipal courts.

The Union Club and the Excelsior Club offered their facilities for use as influenza hospitals, although the short supply of nurses limited the effectiveness of additional hospital space. Cleveland's health commissioner chastised "luxury" nurses, urging them to leave their work and help care for flu victims: "There are hundreds of luxury nurses in the city who do little or nothing and are kept by wealthy families who think they need care for their small troubles. I consider these nurses as much slackers as men who attempt to evade service in the army."

By November 11, the number of new influenza cases had subsided; schools were reopened, and all bans and restrictions ended. Cleveland's death toll stood at 2,223. The city began finding homes for about 400 orphaned children. Unfortunately, influenza returned within two weeks. This milder, but still deadly, version created a new epidemic in late November and into December. On December 6, the United States surgeon general announced that the country did not need to fear a return of the influenza epidemic. On that day, Cleveland reported 170 new cases and 25 deaths. Newspapers offered guidance to help prevent the spread of influenza during the Christmas season. The advice included women avoiding mistletoe and husbands refraining from kissing relatives of their wives, especially targeting the mother-in-law. The second epidemic officially ended after the holiday season, but sporadic occurrences, sometimes fatal, continued until the spring.

Natural causes ended the flu epidemic. Survivors stricken with the disease acquired immunity, as did others who contracted the virus without becoming ill. The influenza virus mutated rapidly, eventually becoming less severe. No cure for the 1918 influenza ever emerged.

THE WATER CURE PHENOMENON

Advertising touted the Spring Cottage and Bathing Establishment's 1836 opening as "a summer retreat from the bustle and cares of business." Located near Lake Erie, north of the current East Fourteenth Street, the enterprise bordered a small stream of sulfur water. Even more opulent "water cure" facilities soon captured both the imaginations and pocketbooks of wealthy Clevelanders. Proponents of water cure treatments believed that submerging portions of a patient's body in cold water for prolonged periods of time would extract blood from diseased parts of the body and, in the process, bring about a cure. These facilities flourished in the second half of the nineteenth century by combining a sanitarium with picturesque surroundings, a resort atmosphere, an abundant source of soft water for treatment and a nearby railroad or streetcar line to provide convenient transportation.

In 1848, Dr. Thomas T. Seelye founded the Cleveland Water Cure Establishment on the outskirts of the city. The rural twenty-four-acre setting (on the south side of Woodland Avenue near the intersection of East Fifty-first Street) encompassed a wooded forest, curving walks, exquisite landscaping and a soft-water spring. Dr. Seelye described the relationship between the beautiful environment and restoration of health with these words: "Ever living springs bubble up from hill and dale in copious profusion to bless the weary, comfort

The Jewish Orphan Asylum took over the old Cleveland Water Cure Establishment (right). A school constructed by the orphan asylum is at left. *Author's collection.*

the distressed, and give health to many a sufferer." While an advertised cost of eight dollars per week included "board, medical advice, and all ordinary attendance of nurses," an actual invoice delineated charges of sixty dollars for two weeks of board, treatment and medicine.

Diaries of two participants provide insights into the methods used. The first patient's treatment included a cold bath in the morning, a walk before breakfast wearing a wet bandage around the chest, a late-morning session in a tub of cold water for twenty minutes and another walk. In midafternoon, the patient retired to bed wrapped in a wet sheet and packed down with three blankets and four comforters. Treatment of some ailments also involved the use of hot water. Major Alexander G. McQueen, the second patient, suffered from chronic diarrhea and bursitis. His morning routine included a bath at a temperature of one hundred degrees for fifteen minutes. The soldier responded well to the treatment during his three-week stay. After leaving the water cure establishment, he suffered a relapse, enduring diarrhea and bursitis for the remainder of his life.

In 1854, following the treatment of more than four hundred patients, the Cleveland Water Cure Establishment expanded its facilities. The enlarged sanitarium ranked among the best in the country. One patient commented, "If a person could not get well in such a place, he deserved to die." Four years later, Dr. Steelye purchased the Forest City Cure, a competing organization located four blocks east at East Fifty-fifth Street and Woodland Avenue. A consolidation of operations resulted in the sale of the 1854 building to the Jewish Orphan Asylum, a transaction producing at least one unexpected consequence. Dr. Steelye, who lived behind the new Orphan Asylum, discovered that orphans would periodically raid his orchards for pears and apples. In 1881, the sanitarium closed shortly after Steelye relocated to Florida.

In 1873, John D. Rockefeller purchased a large tract of land in East Cleveland for investment purposes. He sold ten acres to allow development of the Forest Hill Water Cure Sanitarium, a venture in which he also invested. Two years later, the sanitarium opened on the top of a knoll that provided every room with an exquisite view of Cleveland, Lake Erie or surrounding woodlands. The *Cleveland Leader* predicted that the establishment would "become popular with the best classes of health and pleasure seekers as soon as its attractions are known." But the anticipated success never materialized, partly because a financial panic created an economic depression that lingered into 1877. The next year, Rockefeller repurchased the ten-acre facility to open a private club that

Constructed as a lavish water cure sanitarium, John D. Rockefeller transformed this edifice into Forest Hill, his summer home. *Courtesy of Cleveland Public Library, Photograph Collection.*

remained in business for only one year. The oil tycoon then used the former sanitarium as his own summer home from 1879 through 1915. On December 17, 1917, fire destroyed the mansion.

Dentist Nathan Hardy Ambler understood how to maximize a business opportunity. During the California Gold Rush, he amassed a fortune when his patients used gold dust to pay for his dental services. In 1852, he moved to Cleveland, opened a dental practice and invested in property near Cedar Road, south of University Circle. A natural spring on this acreage contained blue-green water with large amounts of sulfur. Recognizing the economic worth of water thought to be of therapeutic value, he closed the spring to the public and developed a lucrative bottled water business.

Expanding his spring-water interests, Ambler launched in 1880 the Blue Rock Spring Sanitarium. By this time, water cure advocates had accepted hydrotherapy as a treatment for a broad spectrum of ailments ranging from common colds to typhoid fever and insanity. The sanitarium promoted a variety of mineral treatments in baths carved from rock on the ground floor of the building. In 1908, the sanitarium closed as interest in water cure treatments waned. Case Western Reserve University's Emerson Gym is located about where the sanitarium once stood.

In 1898, Dr. Christian Sihler founded the Windsor Institute, the last of Cleveland's major water cure centers. The current Windsor-Laurelwood Hospital in Willoughby is a successor institution. Although a 1910 report by educator Abraham Flexner totally discredited the water cure movement, successful elements of hydrotherapy still exist in treating patients suffering from arthritis, spinal cord injuries, burns, strokes and paralysis.

CLEVELAND'S EXTRAORDINARY SOS

Twentieth-century improvements in water quality and sanitation unwittingly fostered the spread of horrific polio epidemics. Contaminated water and poor hygiene once bestowed on generations of children an early exposure to a mild form of polio. Improved cleanliness and healthier water supplies reduced the chance of acquiring this early immunity, subjecting older children to a much harsher form of the disease. The ultimate triumph over polio, not achieved until the 1960s, required large-scale public inoculations. In this effort, Cleveland served as a model for the nation.

In 1894, the first known polio outbreak in the United States struck 132 people in Vermont. The initial major epidemic, developing during the summer of 1916, affected more than 37,000 people in twenty-six states and resulted in about six thousand deaths and twenty-seven thousand cases of paralysis. From that point, epidemics of various magnitudes appeared nationally nearly every summer, with the most serious polio scourges developing in the 1940s and 1950s.

In 1949, three Boston scientists cultivated a polio virus in laboratory cultures. Prior to this development, researchers believed that the polio virus would only grow in nerve cells of live animals. The discovery led to the development of the first polio vaccine, for which Dr. John F. Enders, Dr. Thomas H. Weller and Dr. Frederick C. Robbins shared a 1954 Nobel Prize. At the time of the award, Dr. Robbins directed the Pediatrics and Contagious Diseases Department at Cleveland Metropolitan General Hospital, along with serving as a professor of Pediatrics at Western Reserve University. Robbins later became dean of Case Western Reserve University's School of Medicine.

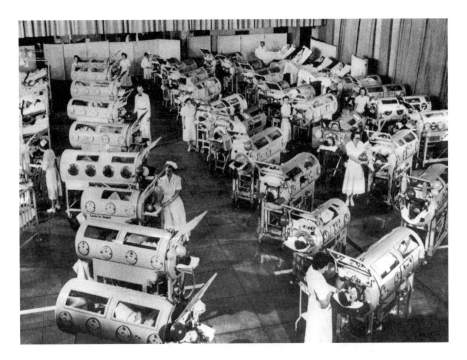

At the height of the polio menace, cylindrical steel drums assisted polio patients with breathing. These "iron lungs" filled entire hospital wards in cities throughout the United States. *Courtesy of Cleveland Public Library, Photograph Collection.*

Prior to the availability of vaccines, fear pervaded families with children as even penicillin, the era's wonder drug, failed to prevent or cure the disease. Concerned parents taped newspaper stories containing warning signs of polio to cupboard doors. The disease proved to be costly as well as terrifying. In the 1950s, the Toomey Pavilion Respiratory Center at City Hospital charged twenty-one dollars per day for physician treatment, medicines and room and board; this cost exceeded an average factory worker's daily earnings.

In 1952, Jonas Salk developed an improved vaccine at the University of Pittsburgh. Three years later, the March of Dimes promoted a mass immunization campaign. The number of polio cases declined by 90 percent in five years. Albert Sabin then developed a vaccine offering significant advantages over the Salk method. Patients received the vaccine dosage orally rather than by needle. The vaccine provided intestinal immunity, which prevented the spread of polio through sewage. Salk's procedure eliminated the possibility of an immune person still transmitting the virus to others. The oral version also promised lifelong immunity.

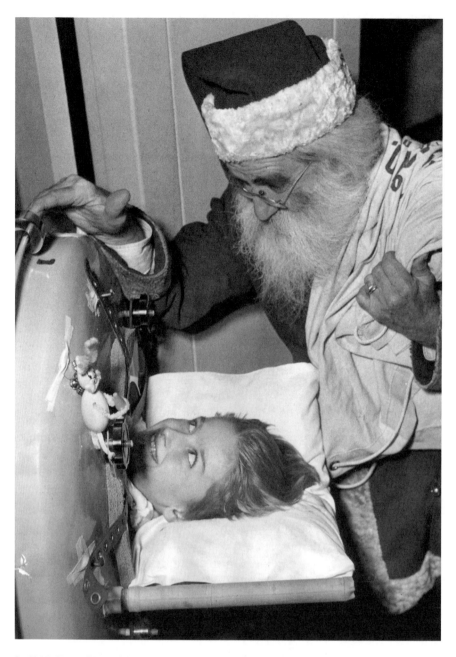

In 1948, Santa Claus visited children in Cleveland City Hospital's polio ward. The victim's head and neck remained outside a sealed, airtight compartment enclosing the remainder of her body. *Courtesy of Cleveland Public Library, Photograph Collection.*

In 1962, Cleveland emerged as America's poster city for promoting and executing large-scale inoculations to prevent polio. Prior to the vaccine's actual availability, Cleveland formulated a "SOS: Sabin Oral Sunday" crusade. Although polio remained a dreaded disease, the SOS promotion required a strong emotional appeal since many people had received protection from the Salk vaccination and no large-scale polio epidemic had occurred in Cleveland for eight years. Cleveland's health officials rose to the challenge of enlisting participation in the SOS endeavor. One week before the first Sunday inoculation, health experts reminded citizens that 10 percent of preschool children had not received protection from the disease. Furthermore, although Cleveland escaped recent epidemics, several large cities did experience outbreaks because people receiving the Salk vaccine could still pass the disease to their children, grandchildren and friends. The Sabin vaccine would eliminate this possibility. Finally, everyone's participation in the SOS effort would permanently end the threat of an epidemic in Cuyahoga County.

Newspapers carried front-page stories and editorials, while movie theaters used trailers to promote the vaccine. Volunteers distributed information about the upcoming initiative to bus riders. SOS posters appeared in retail stores, banks, drugstores, supermarkets, hospitals, barbershops and post offices and on billboards. Bus drivers, teachers and city workers all wore Sabin Oral Sunday badges. Responses to telephone calls for time or weather information began with a message about Sabin Oral Sunday.

Health officials believed that the elimination of local polio epidemics required immunization of 80 percent of Cuyahoga County's population. Every person needed three separate doses, administered at monthly intervals, to combat three different strains of the virus. For each dose, individuals selected one of two consecutive Sundays to receive the inoculation. The mammoth effort of administering vaccines on six separate Sundays required extensive planning, precise logistics and an army of volunteers. A voluntary twenty-five-cent donation helped defray costs, but everyone received the vaccine regardless of his or her ability to contribute.

Cuyahoga County established ninety temporary polio prevention clinics, most of them located in schools. Businesses donated 3,600 pencils for registrations, 748 beer bottle openers to unlock thousands of vaccine containers, ten thousand eyedroppers to measure the vaccine, five hundred cafeteria trays to hold sugar cubes used to consume the vaccine, sixty-five pounds of wire to display informational signs at the sites, five hundred ice cream syrup buckets to store monetary donations, temporary furniture for

In June 1962, volunteers dripped Sabin vaccine onto 5 million sugar cubes donated by grocery chains, a critical step in Cleveland's campaign to eradicate polio epidemics. *Courtesy of Cleveland Public Library, Photograph Collection.*

clinics, coolers with dry ice to transport vaccine from warehouses and IBM tabulators to assist recordkeeping chores. A legion of nearly five thousand volunteers included physicians, pharmacists, pediatricians, dentists, osteopaths, registered nurses and volunteers from the police, Red Cross, Girl Scouts and Boy Scouts. Two warehouses stored about 1 million doses of the vaccine. No city had ever attempted such a massive inoculation.

With the promotion and planning in place, health officials awaited the first day of implementation. A telephone survey indicated that about two-thirds of the population would partake in the program, a cooperation level falling substantially below the 80 percent goal. The actual participation level amazed the entire country.

Day One—Strain 1 (May 27): On the first day, ninety polio prevention clinics operated between noon and 6:00 p.m. Long lines formed almost immediately; some families arrived with picnic baskets. Sports fans carried transistor radios to listen to a Cleveland Indians play-by-play broadcast. While adults chatted with neighbors, children shared new yo-yo tricks with their friends. Pitchmen hawked balloons and souvenirs in a carnival-like atmosphere.

The well-rehearsed vaccine administration plan succeeded in practice. PTA members handled registration forms, while Boy Scouts placed sugar cubes into paper cups. Pharmacists doused the cubes with three drops of the vaccine. Thirty-two ambulances, many donated by undertakers, blasted their sirens as they maneuvered through crowded streets to deliver fresh vaccine supplies from the two warehouses. In total, 882,609 persons received inoculations on the first day. Parma High School, the prevention clinic volume leader, administered 21,390 doses in six hours, an average of 3,565 per hour. Marveling at the first-day results, Albert Sabin told the media, "There has been no record like that anywhere in the world. This is the most extraordinary response I ever have heard of anywhere."

Day Two—Strain 1 (June 2): Between the first and second Sundays, volunteers walked door to door, distributing information in neighborhoods underrepresented in the first week's effort. Logistic improvements included the addition of two new clinics and eight hospitals to augment the two central warehouses. The hospitals ensured that every one of the ninety-two clinics received additional vaccine in fifteen minutes or less. In total, 1,480,429 people (93.5 percent of the Cuyahoga County's population) received protection from the strain 1 virus.

Day Three—Strain 3 (June 24): Only one significant procedural change took place during the second initiative. The focal point for distributing the registration forms shifted to state liquor stores since schools had closed for the summer. Cautiously optimistic health officials realized that a decline in participation could occur during the second round. But 836,188 people responded to the first day of the strain 3 inoculations.

Day Four—Strain 3 (July 1): The response demonstrated Clevelanders' commitment to ending the polio threat. One couple arrived wearing a bridal gown and tuxedo. The newlyweds had just exchanged wedding vows at the Fairmont Temple and stood in line to receive their sugar cubes while en route to their wedding reception. Another family rescheduled a flight to Scotland because the original itinerary interfered with obtaining the vaccine. The two-week total of 1,478,711 individuals receiving the strain 3 vaccine represented 92.9 percent of the target population.

Day Five—Strain 2 (July 22): Cleveland's success during the first two rounds of inoculations generated national attention; an article in *Time* magazine praised Cleveland's successful campaign. Doctors and healthcare officials from across the county visited the city to observe firsthand the logistics of the

SOS initiative. A Sacramento doctor commented, "You'd be a social outcast if you didn't get the vaccine." A Chicago public health official remarked, "It looks like, let's say, a carnival," while a Dallas counterpart observed, "The whole city is going on a picnic." Yet the turnout of 741,765 resulted in the poorest of the three first-day inoculations.

Day Six—Strain 2 (July 29): Clinics opened earlier to accommodate baseball fans headed for a family-day Indians double-header. A large final-day crowd pushed the two-Sunday total to 1,475,361, about 93.4 percent of the population. In total, more than 90 percent of Cuyahoga County's populations received the required three inoculations, demonstrating that such large-scale efforts could succeed.

Locally and nationally, the Salk and Sabin vaccines effectively ended the threat of the dreaded polio epidemics in the United States.

Part VIII

A SCARRED ENVIRONMENT

REVERSING INDUSTRY'S DEADLY LEGACY

Many industrial corporations contributing to Cleveland's growth eventually abandoned the city, leaving a legacy of monumental property misuse. The deserted sites then provided dumping grounds for toxic and hazardous materials. These decaying brownfields consist of land, factories and warehouses sitting vacant because enormous legal liabilities prohibit their reuse. Even banks can be held responsible for lending money to borrowers that fail to complete environmental cleanups. Through the past few decades, imaginative redevelopment proposals have spawned both inspiring triumphs and unpleasant disappointments.

In 1866, a soaring worldwide demand for arc lights triggered the founding of the National Carbon Company in Lakewood, although the business achieved its greatest success in another endeavor. In 1890, responding to demands for portable batteries from the flourishing telephone and fledgling automotive industries, National Carbon became the first mass-producer of industrial batteries. The batteries met the needs of industry but did not satisfy the consumer market's requirements for maintenance-free, durable, non-spill, non-breakable and inexpensive batteries. In response, National Carbon in 1896 marketed the first battery intended for widespread consumer use. The Columbia battery, and its successors, ruled the household market for sixty years until the introduction of alkaline batteries, another Cleveland invention.

An upscale housing development replaced the Eveready facility. The southern border of the Battery Park project blended with early twentieth-century homes across the street. *Courtesy of the author.*

In 1914, National Carbon purchased the American Eveready Corporation and constructed a twenty-building research facility on fourteen acres overlooking Edgewater Park. By the 1950s, the short life of consumer batteries was inhibiting growth of battery-powered household products. In 1959, Lew Urry, an Eveready scientist, revolutionized the industry by developing a long-lasting alkaline battery. In the cafeteria of the Edgewater research complex, he used two toy cars, one equipped with a conventional carbon-zinc battery and the other with his own alkaline battery, to demonstrate the potential of the new invention. The car containing the existing technology traveled only a few feet, while the other, powered by an alkaline battery, raced several laps around the cafeteria. The new battery inspired the manufacture of transistor radios and other consumer goods and paved the way for laptop computers and cellphones. Today, the Smithsonian's National Museum of American History displays prototypes of the alkaline batteries invented in Cleveland, and Lew Urry is a member of the Smithsonian Hall of Fame.

Only two hundred yards from Lake Erie and even closer to Edgewater Beach, the Eveready site endured toxic waste dumping for decades. In 1970, the company even created a large pit to dispose of chemicals, solvents and

Opening in 1874, the Collinwood Rail Yard spawned industrial development in the formerly rural community. The photograph is from 1952. *Author's collection.*

waste oils. Seven years later, the facility closed, although minor operations continued until 1997. The Eveready Company thoroughly cleaned the polluted site and razed the vacant buildings; only a powerhouse once supplying electricity remains standing. In 2007, Battery Park, an upscale housing development consisting of more than 250 townhouses, single-family homes and loft condominiums replaced the old manufacturing site. Still expanding by adding additional homes, Battery Park is a stunning example of conscientious brownfield cleanup and creative reuse.

In the 1870s, vineyards gracing Collinwood's landscape combined with the expansive Collinwood Rail Yard to create the largest shipping point for grapes in the United States. Industrial development accelerated as railroads brought raw materials into factories and transported finished goods to destinations throughout the country. During the Second World War, Collinwood flourished as one of the world's largest centers for industrial production as Fisher Body, Thompson Products, General Electric, Lincoln Electric, Eaton Corporation, National Acme, Bailey Meter and other industrial companies manufactured war products.

Opening in 1921, employment at the Fisher Body Coit Road automobile plant soared to 7,000 in three years. Doubling its number of workers during World War II, the plant produced parts for tanks and B-29 planes. Four decades later, when the plant closed, employment had declined to 1,300 hourly and 400 salaried workers. Responding to a 1988 complaint, the Ohio Environmental Protection Agency discovered hundreds of leaky drums laced with poisonous chemicals, solvents and oils. Thieves pilfering scrap metal exercised little care in handling this polluted material. As a result, hazardous waste contaminated the Nine Mile Creek, a Lake Erie tributary flowing directly through the site. In 1995, demolition of the Fisher Body plant finally ended an appalling era of land and water pollution.

In 1998, the State of Ohio announced a redevelopment plan, anchored by an industrial park slated to attract light and heavy manufacturing companies. Meanwhile, the Job Corps desired a new Cleveland home. The organization offers low-income students a chance to live in a campus setting, allowing them to finish high school, learn a trade and obtain assistance in finding a job. In 2007, the new Collinwood Jobs Corps grounds consisted of dormitories, academic and vocational classrooms, administrative offices and facilities for dining and healthcare. The promise of the anchor industrial park to generate new employment remains unfulfilled.

Kinsman Road begins its southeasterly jaunt at the intersection of East Fifty-fifth Street and Woodland Avenue. The road creates a steadily increasing triangle with the eastern path of Woodland Avenue. Nearby railroads sparked the initial development of this neighborhood. Chemical and paint plants joined lead smelters and other industrial companies in creating nineteenth-century employment. But vanishing jobs after the Second World War plunged the neighborhood into poverty. Widespread deterioration, demolition and illegal dumping caused the area bounded by Kinsman Road, Woodland Avenue and Woodhill Road (East Ninety-third Street) to be nicknamed the "Forgotten Triangle."

Good news, in short supply for decades, sounded more like a miracle when a developer proposed constructing a 352,500-square-foot industrial park at the intersection of East Eightieth Street and Kinsman Road, the exact place where John D. Rockefeller had acquired one of Standard Oil's first refining facilities. But before any meaningful development could take place, a host of major environmental issues needed to be addressed. In response, the State of Ohio provided $3.0 million for site cleanup. Another $1.5 million grant came from Cleveland's Neighborhood Development Investment Fund. The U.S. Environmental Protection Agency's Brownfields Cleanup Revolving Loan Fund supplied a $700,000 low-interest loan.

Rather than create an industrial park, the developer paid $350,000 for the land and subsequently sold it to the Cuyahoga Metropolitan Housing

A Cuyahoga Metropolitan Housing Authority office building enhances Cleveland's "Forgotten Triangle" neighborhood on land where developers promised a new industrial park. *Courtesy of the author.*

Authority for $4.2 million to create an office building. In addition to selling the land at a large profit, the developer received the contract to manage construction of the housing authority's new building. The Forgotten Triangle neighborhood gained an office building but never benefited from the phantom industrial park. The housing authority's new building created no additional jobs, and Cleveland did not gain a penny in new taxes.

Holmden Avenue is sandwiched between Interstate 71 and the Industrial Valley. Backyard views to the east are spectacular, but so is the sharp drop as the land plunges into the valley. Not surprisingly, an officer of a construction management company received a favorable response from three residents when he requested their permission to spread fill dirt, which would partially smooth the rapidly descending terrain. Soon afterward, the soil discolored, an acidic smell filled the air and grass died, as did a nearby willow tree. A 1987 soil test revealed that the backyards contained health-threatening levels of lead and cadmium. The potential health risk developed into a serious concern when the blood of a two-year-old girl, living in one of the homes, contained an above-normal amount of lead.

The company that dumped the dirt worked as an independent contractor to remove soil from a renovation project at the Master Metals Corporation in the Flats. Master Metals extracted lead from batteries and other products, melted the lead into ingots and then sold the ingots. A previous company had performed essentially the same operations at the identical location since 1933.

Fill dirt spread on Holmden Avenue created an environmental controversy. The street is shown near the bottom of its steep, curving drop into Cleveland's Industrial Valley. *Courtesy of the author.*

Master Metals acknowledged that the soil had been hauled from the company's premises. The construction management company official denied ever asking the residents if the dirt could be dumped on their land, claiming that another subcontractor disposed of the dirt. Master Metals countered by claiming that its subcontractor's duties included disposing of the soil at a licensed landfill.

The Ohio Environmental Protection Agency ordered Master Metals to remove the dirt from the Holmden Avenue backyard. The company's first effort, consisting of hauling away one hundred tons of soil, proved inadequate. Two weeks later, the EPA forced Master Metals to remove more dirt. The following spring and autumn, the company carried away hundreds of additional tons of contaminated soil. Meanwhile, as vegetation died on Holmden Avenue, toxic materials attributed to Master Metals emerged in an Aurora dump and a ravine near the Bedford Glens. Once again, Master Metals and subcontracted haulers blamed each other for the problems. Master Metals agreed to remove its waste from the ravine, but the effort stopped after only one day since another 440 cubic yards of solid waste had already been dumped on top of the Master Metals material. The company objected to removing accumulated waste from other companies' illegal activities.

But unlawful dumping turned out to be only the tip of the Master Metals iceberg of environmental abuse. Tests of employees uncovered serious overexposure to airborne lead and arsenic. In 1990, a federal judge ordered workers removed from the plant if their lead levels exceeded federal standards. Unfortunately for Master Metals, the decree encompassed most of the company's forty workers, several of whom registered lead levels doubling the acceptable amount. Outside the plant, lead readings soared twelve times higher than the standard set by both the United States and Ohio EPAs, although officials soon discovered errors in their computations. The Ohio EPA announced that the lead levels actually exceeded national standards by more than 2,300 percent.

Plagued by a combination of federal, state and city regulators, Master Metals agreed to close its operations for thirty days to bring pollution levels under control. One year after reopening, lead levels still exceeded national air-quality standards by 973 percent. The Ohio Environmental Protection Agency ordered an immediate shutdown of the plant, after which the company closed.

In 1997, following a partial cleanup of the vacant Master Metals site, lead and other toxic metals remained at concentrations as much as thirty-five times higher than Environmental Protection Agency standards. Although not reusable, the land did not pose an immediate threat to the surrounding environment, so the prime industrial site sat barren, unused and uncleaned. Local and state leaders persuaded the Environmental Protection Agency to revise the cleanup plan to permit future development. The modified strategy called for removal of lead-contaminated soil, razing of several buildings and covering the site with asphalt. In 2003, the Northern Ohio Lumber and Timber Company, with a local history dating back to the 1860s, moved 1.5 miles from its Carter Road location to the old Master Metals site. A brownfield originally possessing little chance of successful reclamation is now being productively used by the lumber company.

A RADIOACTIVE NEIGHBORHOOD

Only a mile apart, two industrial operations on Harvard Avenue secretly processed uranium for all but five of the twenty-nine years spanning 1944 through 1972. Nearby neighborhood residents endured exposure to uranium that hindered their health. The operations even physically wrecked

The 3,232-foot Harvard-Denison Bridge spanned the Cuyahoga River and Industrial Valley. The Harshaw Chemical Company, shown in 1954, secretly processed uranium below the bridge. *Courtesy of Special Collections, Michael Schwartz Library, Cleveland State University.*

a three-thousand-foot bridge. Today, children safely frolic in a playground constructed on one of the formerly contaminated sites.

For sixty years, the majestic Harvard-Denison Bridge towered over Cleveland's Industrial Valley. Below the bridge, on the bank of the Cuyahoga River, a Harshaw Chemical Company factory had produced specialty chemicals since the early 1900s. In the 1940s, the Atomic Energy Commission subcontracted Harshaw to supply research and production support for the development and manufacture of atomic bombs. The company chose the Cuyahoga River plant as its production facility.

Harshaw's primary assignment consisted of refining uranium oxide (yellow cake) into uranium orange oxide, although the company also converted other oxides as well. Uranium powder arrived by train from Colorado, New York, Pennsylvania and Canada. Workers removed impurities, refined the compounds and sent the uranium to Oak Ridge, Tennessee, for additional processing. By 1948, Harshaw ranked as one of the nation's largest producers of uranium compounds. The production, in combination with Cleveland's humid summer air, created hydrofluoric acid as a byproduct. The acid's fumes corroded the Harvard-Denison Bridge's steel structure beyond repair.

Within the plant, window glass decayed, while workers' leather shoes disintegrated, events suggesting that employees could also be at risk. In

Although shielding themselves from fumes, people living near the Harvard-Denison Bridge did not realize that their pollution challenges also included radioactivity. *Courtesy of Special Collections, Michael Schwartz Library, Cleveland State University.*

2000, *USA Today* published a three-part report concerning the early Cold War nuclear program. The newspaper cited classified information implying that Harshaw employees' exposure to uranium dust greatly exceeded amounts considered safe, thus increasing risks of cancer, kidney ailments and respiratory problems.

Employees received a different story. If fact, a government report praised workers' unusually healthy and physically sound condition, attributing their fitness to the uranium exposure. According to the government's logic, uranium fumes killed nearby bacteria, thus making employees less likely to contract colds, infections and commonplace illnesses. Meanwhile, pollution spread outside the complex. Atomic Energy Commission officials repeatedly warned Harshaw, in classified documents, about potential uranium problems.

In the early 1950s, the company abruptly removed workers from production activities after analyzing urine tests. In 1951, nine workers contracted kidney ailments attributed to uranium poisoning. The following year, classified letters from Harshaw to the Atomic Energy Commission documented difficulties with converting orange oxide to brown oxide. The problems included leaking equipment, spills and emission releases into the environment.

In 1959, the Atomic Energy Commission ended its work with Harshaw, releasing the plant for general use. The plant continued to produce chemicals until 1994. Five buildings remain on the site, but only a warehouse is in current use. Investigations indicated that traces of yellow cake still exist but create no immediate threat to human health or to the environment. The conclusion of Harshaw's involvement with the Atomic Energy Commission provided a five-year respite from uranium processing in the neighborhood.

In 1965, the Chemetron Corporation's Harvard Avenue plant began manufacturing an antimony oxide catalyst using depleted uranium not strong enough to directly penetrate the body. But the uranium could be introduced into the body by breathing or through the skin. The site recorded unacceptable levels of radioactivity long after processing ceased in 1972.

In addition, Chemetron owned a ten-acre landfill on Bert Avenue in Newburgh Heights, three blocks north of the Harvard Avenue plant. Neighbors, learning of Chemetron's activities with uranium processing, asked the United States Nuclear Regulatory Commission to examine the dump. A 1980 investigation discovered traces of radiation existing in ground samples, probably occurring because the company transported

This Harvard Avenue plant used depleted uranium in its production process. During the Second World War, the facility became one of the first napalm suppliers. *Courtesy of Diane Dutka.*

contaminated rubble from the Harvard Avenue plant to the landfill in 1975. Unrelated to the uranium issue, the investigation uncovered traces of trichloroethylene, a potentially deadly chemical if inhaled, ingested or absorbed through the skin. Once used in food production and as a solvent for dry cleaning and metal degreasing, the chemical is commonly found in hundreds of waste sites. This constituted enough evidence to warrant cleanup of the landfill.

After years of delay, the Sunbeam/Oster Company inherited responsibility for the cleanup through a series of business mergers and purchases. The company's conscientious cleanup effort permitted continued use of chemical processing operations. The Nuclear Regulatory Commission eventually released the manufacturing plant and landfill for unrestricted use. A playground resides on the former landfill site.

BROADWAY'S BROWNFIELD INFERNO

Opened in 1902, the Worsted Mills and a predecessor business employed thousands of immigrants and unskilled workers since 1878. Evolving into an 8.5-acre plant, the mill consumed three Broadway Avenue blocks a short distance south of the road's intersection with East Fifty-fifth Street.

Employing about 2,500 workers in 1920, the business ranked among the largest worsted mills in the country.

After receiving wool from sheep ranches throughout the world, Worsted Mill employees manually graded and scrubbed the incoming fleece before sending the wool to cleaning and drying equipment. A series of machines blended fibers, straightened the wool, eliminated shorter and weaker fibers, created balls of fiber and developed a uniformly strong product for the spinning process. The mill targeted the longest and strongest fibers for production of Worsted material. Woolens, produced chiefly from short wool and reworked scrap, developed into the raw material for blankets, flannels and other fabric of lesser quality. Machines spun the finest fiber into yarn,

Between 1902 and 1956, the Worsted Mills on Broadway Avenue provided work for thousands of Clevelanders. *Courtesy of Cleveland Public Library, Photograph Collection.*

which looms then wove into cloth. After a thorough inspection, a plant in Ravenna performed dyeing and finishing operations requiring clean water; the company purchased two nearby lakes to ensure a daily supply of more than two million gallons of pure water. Clothing manufacturers purchased the finished woven Worsted cloth as the material used in the finest suits, dresses and other garments.

The Worsted Mills neighborhood acquired the flavor of the Czech, Pole and Lithuanian immigrants working in the mill. Employees walked to work, so modest homes surrounded the plant. Restaurants, clubs and bars catered to the need for relaxation after toiling long hours at the plant. Nearby churches, banks, doctors' offices, barbershops, drugstores and scores of other service businesses thrived, while the plant itself housed a seven-hundred-seat cafeteria, a library, a dispensary and a set of bowling alleys.

A grueling six-day, fifty-five-hour workweek encompassed weekday operations from 7:00 a.m. to 5:00 p.m., as well as a five-hour Saturday shift from 7:00 a.m. to noon. Weekend chores included cleaning equipment and polishing the buildings' oak floors. Inspectors checked the work, awarding prizes, often a cup of ice cream in the cafeteria, to employees creating the most pristine environment. The company even displayed a banner identifying the workplace as the cleanest for the week.

In the 1920s, a skilled worker earned twelve dollars per week, while an apprentice received half that amount. In addition, experienced workers received a one-cent bonus for each perfect yard produced. Wages dropped to seven dollars per week during the Depression. In the mid-1930s, the company increased productivity by investing in new equipment. In 1937, employees staged an unsuccessful three-month strike to obtain union representation. By the mid-1940s, pay had increased to forty-five dollars per week. In 1946, the Warner & Swasey Company, located about three miles from the Worsted Mills, initiated research culminating in the first projectile looms. In 1952, the Worsted Mills installed eight of these new looms, doubling the cloth produced per machine. Pay increased to sixty dollars for a forty-hour workweek.

In 1955, employees selected the Textile Workers Union of America to represent them in contract negotiations. On August 22, 1955, workers walked off their jobs after failing to attain a 7.5-cent-per-hour wage increase. None of the strikers ever worked at the Worsted Mills again. After the labor stoppage dragged on for months without a settlement, shareholders elected to liquidate the company. Rumors of the impending closing propelled the stock from $89 per share in December to $137 at the time the plant ceased

In 1949, Worsted Mill employees performed most of the tasks required to transform sheep wool into material for clothing. *Courtesy of Cleveland Public Library, Photograph Collection.*

business on January 18, 1956. The price increase reflected management's conservative operations. The Worsted Mill's assets totaled about $20 million, much of it in very liquid securities. Liabilities amounted to less than $1 million. Stockholders ultimately received about $18 million when the company dissolved.

To the casual observer, the fourteen-building complex appeared abandoned for decades. But nineteen small businesses used a few of the old structures as warehouses. In 1991, tenants set in motion a series of events leading to the eventual destruction of the entire facility. The businesses complained to the city that their water had been disconnected because the owner failed to pay utility bills. Inspectors, sent by the city to investigate the water shutoff, observed illegal storage of hazardous waste and a multitude of safety violations. The Ohio Environmental Protection Agency later discovered about two hundred drums of illegally stored waste materials. Fire and safety hazards included blocked fire exits, sprinklers not in working order and other dangerous conditions.

The City of Cleveland filed a complaint in Municipal Housing Court claiming that the property constituted a public nuisance. A concurring judge ordered the tenants to vacate the grounds and demanded that the owners bring all buildings into compliance with fire and health codes. Forcing owners to clean the environmental mess proved problematic because neither the city nor the courts could conclusively determine who actually owned the buildings. The site once experienced a change in ownership five times within an eight-month period. A pair of California businesses, owned by the same person, each purchased and sold the complex. At two different times, the property had been sold twice on the same day. Eventually, the city concluded that California-based MPC-Barton Corporation, also known as Premier Enterprises, owned the buildings about the time of the 1991 inspection. But Premier Enterprises soon filed for bankruptcy protection.

In 1993, two Cuyahoga County grand juries investigated violations of environmental law at the complex. The first jury spent several largely unproductive months attempting to determine the current and past owners of the buildings. The second jury concentrated on establishing responsibility; this focus eventually resulted in indictments, convictions and court orders to clean the plant.

On July 4, 1993, a spectacular fire, set by arsonists, engulfed most of the complex. Eyewitness reported two individuals running from the site just before the blaze erupted, cautioning bystanders to quickly leave because of an impending inferno. The resulting conflagration is considered one of Cleveland's worst fires. Because of extreme heat, the fire department's water vaporized long before it reached its intended target. One of the buildings collapsed onto Broadway Avenue, downing traffic lights and power lines. Broadway Avenue, the neighborhood's busiest thoroughfare, remained closed for two days. The fire traveled across the street, temporarily displacing twenty-one families living in an apartment building. Burning for three days, the heat melted the vinyl siding on an apartment and destroyed surrounding buildings.

The United States Bureau of Alcohol, Tobacco and Firearms sent a fourteen-person arson team to investigate the fire, but responsibility for the inferno remains a mystery. Finally cleared of fire debris and hazardous waste, the site now is the home of a Cleveland Boys and Girls Club. Opened in 2002, the facility includes a twenty-seven-thousand-square-foot building containing a gymnasium, classrooms and administrative offices. A little league baseball diamond and a football/soccer field are part of the campus. The club is aiding the rejuvenation of a once thriving but deteriorating neighborhood.

A FOUNDATION OF GARBAGE

As the twenty-first century dawned, the still attractive city of Garfield Heights needed an infusion of new vitality. Once a flourishing inner ring Cleveland suburb, the city stagnated as its population matured and its housing and business stock aged. In 2001, developers and the City of Garfield Heights announced what appeared to be a perfect panacea for the suburb's doldrums: a set of multiple projects encompassing office buildings, big-box retailers, restaurants and hotels. In total, about $1 billion would be spent on new development convenient to Garfield Heights, adjoining suburbs, parts of residential Cleveland, the airport and downtown Cleveland. Situated directly south of I-480, even more shoppers would be drawn from the 180,000 motorists traveling the freeway each workday.

Although promising to rejuvenate Garfield Heights, the projects faced a significant challenge; parts of the sites once housed a landfill, with waste buried to depths exceeding one hundred feet. Since Ohio did not regulate landfills until 1968, little information existed regarding the amount and nature of the garbage buried beneath the proposed new development. Although the dump closed in the 1970s, methane gas, created when bacteria in decaying garbage are deprived of oxygen, continued to form into the twenty-first century.

Methane issues in nearby neighborhoods had sparked controversies for decades. On the more spectacular side, the Harvard Refuse Landfill, near Warner Road, released methane gas that penetrated a sewer on New York Avenue. Somewhat complementing noisy Independence Day festivities, the sewer exploded on July 4, 1986. Residents, fearing that their homes might be next to detonate, received little assurance to the contrary when inspectors discovered combustible levels of methane in three residences near the landfill.

In 2004, construction started on the first phase of one of Garfield Height's mega-projects, a $70 million, 650,000-square-foot retail shopping complex named City View. While property situated on abandoned landfills had been successfully converted into parks, jogging paths and golf courses, neither the developers nor the Ohio Environmental Protection Agency possessed expertise in special requirements unique to construction of a retail complex. The initial excavation consisted of removing about 48.6 million cubic feet of combined earth and trash, which, according to EPA regulations, must remain somewhere on the site. Consequently, an immense quantity of earth and fermenting garbage

Vegetation grows on Transportation Boulevard's soil-covered garbage mound, a byproduct of the City View strip mall construction. *Courtesy of the author.*

(measuring 60 feet in height, 1,100 feet in length and 400 feet in width) found a new home overlooking the strip mall under construction.

The giant heap quickly created an aroma of garbage, triggering headaches, nosebleeds and fatigue among residents, construction workers and guests. The stench prevailed even after the builder sprayed the mound with cherry-scented water. The developer promised to cover the mound with landscaping and a pavilion offering spectacular views of the Cuyahoga Valley, but the garbage pile seemed intent on implementing its own plans. As the miniature mountain of debris collapsed, parts of the heap started moving directly toward a fully occupied office building. Although the garbage did not quite reach its apparent target, property infringement caused construction delays and EPA fines. Employees at the office facility complained that daily exposure to odors had created a permanent smell within the interiors of their parked automobiles.

After the garbage mound's movement abated, attention focused on two significant construction challenges. The first task involved preventing the complex from sinking into the landfill. Since a quarry once occupied the site, bedrock could be used as a base. Construction crews sank anchors and about 2,500 steel pilings deep into the decaying garbage. The second issue concerned the ultimate safety of the new complex. Without proper venting, methane gas could easily explode. A layer of clay, ranging from three to seven feet, acted as a methane barrier. Constructing the barrier required hauling and spreading more than 1 million cubic yards of clay and then creating a one-foot bed of gravel as a topping. Pipes placed in the clay trapped methane and vented it to the open air above the buildings' rooftops. The developer also installed methane sensors throughout the complex.

Bed, Bath and Beyond, the first store to open in the new strip mall, unlocked its doors in February 2006. Anchored by Walmart, retailers fully occupied the mall by September. But before 2006 ended, sounds of methane alarms resulted in store evacuations and 105 visits from the fire department. Although no dangerous levels of methane had been discovered, the sensitive alarms caused shopper inconvenience and uneasiness. A defective floor drain tripped an alarm at Walmart, and faulty heating set off a siren at the A.J. Wright Company. An aerosol-propelled dog grooming product seemed to be the culprit at PetSmart, while cleaning products activated alarms at the Sally Beauty Supply site. An alleged malfunctioning sensor resulted in evacuation of a Giant Eagle grocery store.

Environmental problems persisted and worsened. Whatever the reason, customers thought that the Walmart store discharged a smell similar to rotten eggs. Actual detection of methane gas during the heavy-volume Christmas season forced evacuation and the closing of Walmart for two days. A methane alarm sounded on Christmas Eve at a Jo-Ann Fabrics store. While the actual risk of an explosion remained controversial, alarms and evacuations did nothing to enhance the shopping experience or confidence in the mall's safety.

In December 2007, customer confidence worsened when a spark from a paving machine ignited a methane fire in City View's parking lot. A month later, the Ohio EPA halted construction of three nearby buildings that did not contain the required clay capping. The next spring, EPA inspectors discovered explosive levels of methane gas in sewer basins under City View's parking lots and in a nearby mound of dirt-covered garbage. The developer accused the EPA of maneuvering to obtain a bargaining advantage in settling remaining issues. Three months later, the EPA did more than maneuver. The Ohio attorney general filed a twenty-five-count lawsuit charging the owners and operators of the shopping center, along with the City of Garfield Heights, with violating state pollution laws.

In 2008, just twenty-five months after its City View opening, Walmart cited safety issues in pulling out of the complex. Its departure triggered a mass exodus of retailers. Today, only a Giant Eagle grocery store and an OfficeMax outlet remain in the otherwise abandoned strip mall. After selling City View less than two years following its opening, the original

Immediately following a successful Giant Eagle grocery store, only an OfficeMax outlet remains in this barren strip mall accompanied by a desolate parking lot. *Courtesy of the author.*

developer filed for bankruptcy. A new owner promptly defaulted on mortgage payments.

Meanwhile, unpaid contractors walked off the site of Bridgeview Crossing, a planned strip mall and office complex located west of City View. Weeds, abandoned construction materials and skeletons of buildings sit on a ninety-acre site that Lowe's, Target, JCPenney and an Aldi grocery store once planned to occupy. No office buildings or hotels have been constructed, but a smaller retail strip mall south of Bridgeview Crossing has successfully operated with a mix of retail stores and casual dining establishments.

ABOUT THE AUTHOR

Native Clevelander Alan Dutka is a retired executive. During his business career, he authored four marketing research books, including *Customer Satisfaction Research*, a primary selection of the Newbridge Executive Book Club that has been translated into Spanish and Japanese editions. Since his retirement, he has published three other Cleveland history books: *East Fourth Street: The Rise, Decline, and Rebirth of an Urban Cleveland Street*; *Cleveland's Short Vincent: The Theatrical Grill and Its Notorious Neighbors*; and *Cleveland in the Gilded Age: A Stroll Down Millionaires' Row* (coauthored with Dan Ruminski). Dutka has appeared on the *Feagler & Friends* and *Applause* television shows, along with radio programs including Dee Perry's *Around Noon* and Jacqueline Gerber's morning program. He is a popular speaker at historical societies, libraries and community centers.